DICKENS AT GAD'S HILL

To all members of the Dickens Fellowship, past and present, by whose vigilance and efforts, numerous places associated with Charles Dickens have been preserved for posterity.

The Geranium

Charles Dickens had written as the final line to his story The Haunted Man, "Lord keep my memory green." It is interesting to recall why the geranium, bright in scarlet and green, is kept freshly watered as the emblem flower of the Dickens Fellowship.

The story is this, between the years 1828 and 1836, the geranium in all its varied species, became the most popular flower in Victorian England. Even the children used it – in a game in which a forfeit was demanded if a leaf of geranium could not be produced. The Dickens' children may have learned the game, first of all, when the family stayed in Italy.

By the time the gardens at Gad's Hill Place were planted, geraniums were de rigeur, regimented into borders edged with lobelia and sweet alyssum. In France the geranium was circled with cedum and begonias, in Germany by pansies. Petunias and geraniums filled the smartest window boxes, and on massive dining tables geraniums were artistically mixed with nastursiums in small glass cups. At which thought the modern flower arrangers will no doubt boggle.

Charles Dickens loved the brilliance of colour, not only in gardens but on his own person. He and Count D'Orsay were considered leaders of fashion in the matter of richly embroidered waistcoats and so on. He used to speak of a certain coat lined with geranium-red satin which the family felt to be "too much of a good thing" – they persuaded him to abandon it.

At Gad's Hill my great aunt Kitty (the second daughter) laughingly told papa that when he became an angel he would wear a wreath of geraniums and have wings of bright mirror glass. He loved mirrors all round his rooms.

The suitability of the flower as a Dickensian bloom goes back, too, to the old lost languages of flowers, much in fashion during his time, and the meanings of the various geraniums seem to me to reflect the character of Dickens perfectly.

The scarlet geranium means comfort, and my great aunt Mamie (the eldest daughter) often spoke of the writer's gift of comfort. She wrote: "his was a tender and most affectionate nature."

The oak-leaved geranium means true friendship, a quality made plain in his own letters and in many of the biographies, which show the warmth and lasting friendship given to a great variety of people.

The lemon-scented geranium means an unexpected meeting and the nutmeg geranium an expected meeting, Charles Dickens rejoyced in such events.

A dark geranium means melancholy and he certainly had moods of near despair and heavy oppression. How else could he have depicted such emotions so feelingly?

While composing the final scenes for Little Nell's death, he wrote: "I went to bed utterly dispirited and done up. All night I have been pursued by the child and this morning I am unrefreshed and miserable."

The ivy-leaved geranium means "bridal flavour" and Dickens dearly loved a happy wedding day, even bringing much humour into the grim occasion when Mr Dombey married Edith.

Even the small wild geranium has its place, for it means religious piety. In 1849, in his own handwriting with the usual quill pen and blue ink, he wrote a simple version of the scriptures called "The Life of Our Lord" expressly for his own children.

The geranium – from the Greek for crane, referring to the seed being like the bill of that bird – is also called dove-foot, cranesbill and alumroot, and the plant has tonic qualities, a pungent scent, and is sturdy, varied and prolific.

How right that it should be the favourite for those who wish to keep Dickens' memory green!

Did you ever put a leaf of the sweet scented geranium under a sponge cake before baking it? It is quite delicious – that cake.

Mrs Stuart McHugh

DICKENS
AT
GAD'S HILL

by
ALAN S. WATTS
Honorary General Secretary,
The Dickens Fellowship

FACSIMILE OF CHARLES DICKENS' BOOK-PLATE

First published 1989 by Cedric Dickens and Elvendon
Press, The Old Surgery, High Street, Goring-on-Thames,
Reading, Berkshire RG8 9AW.

Designed by P Squared Design
Typeset by Joshua Associates Ltd, Oxford
Printed in England by The Bath Press, Avon

ISBN 0 906 552 42 7 (hardback edition)
ISBN 0 906 552 43 5 (paperback edition)

Contents

GUINNESS, AS GOOD NOW AS IT WAS IN 1837
Cedric Dickens

"A LARGE HAMPER OF GUINNESS'S STOUT"

" The chattels of Mrs. Bloss were forwarded by instalments. First there came a large hamper of Guinness's stout and an umbrella . . . "

LATER

" ' Married! ' cried Mrs. Bloss, taking the pill and a draught of Guinness—' Married! Unpossible! ' "

(From 'Sketches by Boz')

Guinness is brewed today from the same ingredients, and by essentially the same methods, as in 1836, when 'Boz' published his Sketches—and for that matter in 1759, when Guinness was first brewed in Dublin. It is as good for us as it was for our great-great-great grandfathers.

GUINNESS IS GOOD FOR YOU

This advertisement appeared in the Summer 1955 Dickensian

Foreword

Ever since he was a small boy, Charles Dickens had dreamed that he might one day live at Gad's Hill Place, on the Old Dover Road near Rochester.

His dream was realised in 1855 when he bought the house and some twenty-six acres for £1,700, and lived in it, off and on, for fifteen years.

He loved Gad's Hill, although the years after he moved in were difficult and turbulent, with the estrangement and separation from his wife, the death of his son Walter in India, the extravagance and debts of other sons, and the onset of his heart and circulation problems, with bouts of depression, betrayed by an increasing sombreness in his later books.

Nevertheless, with his great energy and passion for life, his years here were full and productive. He did some of his best work, in his study and in the chalet in the wilderness across the road. He roamed over the countryside on horse or foot. He loved to be the genial country squire, running local cricket matches, giving spectacular Christmas parties, and filling the comfortable guest rooms with friends old and new, like Longfellow and the demanding Hans Andersen, who came for two weeks and stayed for five, to the disgust of the unimpressed Dickens family.

Gad's Hill, the first place he owned, is perhaps the most important of Charles Dickens' houses. Here he wrote much of *A Tale of Two Cities*, *Great Expectations*, *Our Mutual Friend*, and *The Mystery of Edwin Drood*. Here he learned to love the countryside as much as he loved London. Here, after the exhausting reading tours all over this country and America, he came home to peace and security, and here, in the middle of Chapter 22 of *Edwin Drood*, his life ended, at the age of 58.

Monica Dickens

ACKNOWLEDGMENTS

I would like to thank Mr Cedric Dickens for encouraging me to write this little book; Mr John Grinstead ARCA for information about the former occupants of Gad's Hill Place; Dr David Parker and Miss Emma Shackleton for their assistance with the illustrations; and the Rt. Rev. Michael Dickens Whinney for permission to use extracts from an article by Mary Angela Dickens. Finally, I should like to thank Miss Catherine Noonan for typing the manuscript.

All extracts from Dickens' letters have been taken from *The Nonesuch Edition*.

A.S.W.

CHAPTER 1

Gad's Hill
and the House Thereon

"This is Falstaff's Gad's Hill, and I live on the top of it," wrote Dickens to the Earl of Carlisle.

Today we might be tempted to regard it primarily as Dickens' Gad's Hill, and neglect its long and interesting history before Dickens ever set eyes on it.

No doubt it was originally God's Hill. There are places in England which still bear this name, and there is at least one other Gads Hill. Certainly this high ground between Gravesend and Rochester was known as Gadshill in Shakespeare's day, and possibly also in Chaucer's. As a hill it is hard to define. It is a summit of a long ascent from the river, rather than a definite hillock. Strood Hill to the East, by which the highway descends to Rochester, is much steeper, and travellers journeying towards London might well have been out of breath once they reached the top. This would explain the remark by Shakespeare's First Traveller in *Henry IV, Part I*: "Come, neighbours; the boy shall lead our horses down the hill; we'll walk afoot awhile, and ease our legs." They were, as we have been told earlier in the play, "riding to London with fat purses". In another minute Falstaff and his companions set upon them, the fat knight shouting: "Strike! Down with them! Cut the villains' throats: ah, whoreson caterpillars! bacon-fed knaves! they hate us youth: down with them; fleece them!"

This scene had been familiar to Dickens since childhood, and he delighted in the fact that this exciting episode had supposedly been enacted within walking distance of his home in Chatham. For he was well aware of the sequel, how Prince Hal and Poins had cunningly detached themselves from Falstaff's party in order to don a disguise and rob the robbers, and how Falstaff had called the Prince and Poins "two arrant cowards", adding: "There's no more valour in that Poins than in a wild duck." No sooner had he said this, however, than Falstaff was assailed by two masked men, and without giving more than token resistance, had fled leaving all the booty in their hands.

In the *Uncommercial Traveller* paper entitled 'Travelling Abroad', Dickens imagined himself on this stretch of road meeting the "very queer small boy" who had been himself:

> "Presently, the very queer small boy says, 'This is Gads-hill we are coming to, where Falstaff went to rob those travellers, and ran away.'
> 'You know something about Falstaff, eh?', said I.
> 'All about him,' said the very queer small boy."

It was a notoriously dangerous place. It was strongly suspected that some of the servants at the Rochester inns worked hand-in-glove with the foot-pads and highwaymen, just as Shakespeare described the Chamberlain passing on information to Master Gadshill: "It holds current that I told you yesternight. There's a franklin in the wild of Kent hath brought three hundred marks with him in gold. I heard him tell it to one of his company last night at supper." Something of that sort might have happened at the Rochester inn where Duke Frederick of Würtemburg stayed in 1592. "Afterwards," wrote the chronicler of his *Visit*, "his Highness rode back again to Gravesend, the night being as dark as pitch and the wind high and boisterous; he slept there that night. On the road, however, an Englishman, with a drawn sword in his hand, came upon us unawares and ran after us as fast as he could; perhaps he expected to find other persons, for it is very probable that he had an ambush, as that particular part of the road is not the most safe."

This second half of the 16th Century seems to have been a particularly bad time for robberies in this locality. F.G. Kitton pointed out that in 1558 a ballad was published entitled *The Robbery at Gad's Hill*, and quoted the Chief Baron of the Exchequer, Sir Roger Manwood, saying in 1590, "Many robberies were done in the bye-ways at Gadeshill . . . by horse-thieves, with such fat and lusty horses as were not like hackney horses, nor far-journeying horses . . . and no man durst travel that way without great company."

This warning was not observed by the Prince of Transylvania who came to England in 1661 on a mission to Charles II.

Prince Cossuma Albertus was on his way home when, in the ascent of Gad's Hill, his coach stuck fast in the mire. Efforts to free it having failed, and night descending, the Prince decided to stay where he was until morning and sleep inside the coach. Just after midnight he was surprised by the coachman and a footman who stabbed him in the heart, dragged him outside and cut off his head. The crime was not discovered for some days, until a Rochester doctor out riding, saw that his dog was intent upon something in a ditch. When the dog pulled out a human arm, the horrified doctor was led to discover the remainder of the Prince's body.

His murderers were not long being traced. They had taken the coach and left it at Greenhithe before setting off for London. There they were arrested, tried, and hanged.

Fifteen years later, in 1676, a so-called 'gentleman of the road' named Swift Nicks Nevisham was operating in this vicinity. One morning at 4 o'clock, so the story goes, he waylaid and robbed a traveller at Gad's Hill. He thereupon rode north to the River Thames which he crossed by ferry. He carried on riding, never pausing, unless possibly to change horses, until he reached York. There he presented himself on the bowling green. Then, seeing the Mayor of York, he boldly went up to him and asked what time of day it was. When subsequently he was arrested for the robbery and put on trial, he called the mayor to testify to the time and date when he had been in York. Not surprisingly, the jury, deeming a ride from Gadshill to York all in one day an impossibility, returned a verdict of "Not Guilty". The story, true or not, probably furnished Dickens' friend, Harrison Ainsworth, with the idea of Dick Turpin's ride to York which was the principal episode in his novel *Rookwood*.

It is interesting that Poins, organising the Falstaff adventure, decided to strike at the same time in the early morning as Nevisham: "But, my lads, my lads, tomorrow morning, by four o'clock, early at Gadshill! There are pilgrims going to Canterbury with rich offerings, and traders riding to London with fat purses." Shakespeare thus drew attention to the two-way traffic on the road, the merchants bound for London and the pilgrims going to Canterbury. There would have been fewer pilgrims in Shakespeare's day. With the Reformation, the magnificent shrine of St. Thomas à Becket had been demolished. However, in this play Shakespeare was writing of the mediaeval world of Henry IV when the roads would still be crowded with pilgrims once April with its sweet showers arrived and the season for pilgrimages came around again.

This brings to mind that Gadshill is not only associated with Shakespeare and Dickens, but with their predecessor in the same tradition, Geoffrey Chaucer. The twenty-nine pilgrims who set out from the Tabard Inn in Southwark (not far from where the Marshalsea Prison later stood) under the guidance of Mine Host, Harry Bailly, would all have qualified as Dickens characters. On their journey to Canterbury, they must have struggled up the long ascent to Gad's Hill. The exertion might well have put a stop to their story-telling for a while until they regained their breath at the top, and it is a pleasant thought to imagine them – the Knight, the Prioress, the Miller, and Chaucer himself – sitting on the sward where Gad's Hill Place now stands while their variety of mounts cropped the grass and the bustling Harry Bailly made arrangements for the next tale to be told.

This is perhaps no idle imagining. If the Canterbury Pilgrims came up Gad's Hill, as they assuredly did, they must have done what other travellers did for years to come – pause at the top. Dickens has attested to the truth of this. In his *Uncommercial* paper on 'Tramps' he wrote: "I have my eye upon a piece of Kentish road, bordered on either side by a wood, and having on the one hand, between the road-dust and the trees, a skirting patch of grass. Wild flowers grow in abundance on this spot, and it lies high and airy, with a distant river stealing steadily way to the ocean, like a man's life. To gain the milestone here, which the moss, primroses, violets, blue-bells, and wild roses, would soon render illegible but for peering travellers pushing them aside with their sticks, you must come up a steep hill, come which way you may. So, all the tramps with carts or caravans – the Gipsy-tramp, the Show-tramp, the Cheap Jack – find it impossible to resist the temptations of the place, and all turn the horse loose when they come to it, and boil the pot."

This was the Old Dover Road which had not only seen pilgrims and merchants going to and fro, but the comings and goings of ambassadors, legates, prelates, royal brides, kings returning from exile, couriers bearing vital dispatches, and young gentlemen and their tutors setting forth on their Grand Tour. The later traffic on the road is described by Mrs. Lynn Linton, from whom Dickens purchased Gad's Hill Place. She recalled the time when she resided there: "Between seventy and eighty coaches, vans, and mail-carts passed our house during the day, besides private carriages, specially those of travellers posting to and from Dover. Regiments, too, often passed on their way to Gravesend, where they embarked for India; and ships' companies, paid off, rowdy and half-tipsy, made the road really dangerous for the time being."

This was that Dover road which had lain, "one Friday night late in November", before the first of the persons with which *A Tale of Two Cities* had its business, and on which, throughout that night "the mail-coach lumbered, jolted, rattled, and bumped upon its tedious way" bearing Mr. Jarvis Lorry on the first stage of his journey to Paris. It was also the road along which a faster coach, in better weather, had sped with four gullible Pickwickians upon its roof, listening avidly to the amazing adventures of Mr. Alfred Jingle. They might indeed have passed a weary little boy, with no waistcoat, and no luggage, trudging along, getting through three and twenty miles on the straight road during the second day of his journey and making for Chatham where he would creep upon "a sort of grass-grown battery overhanging a lane, where a sentry was walking to and fro". But the Pickwickians were too engrossed with Mr. Jingle, and when the coach changed horses, were too anxious to refresh themselves with glasses of ale to notice David Copperfield.

They might well have refreshed themselves at "a delightfully old-fashioned roadside inn of the coaching days ... which no man possessed of a penny was ever known to pass in warm weather." This was, and is, the Sir John Falstaff, a hostelry on the north side of the road a little below Dickens' house. It was used by Dickens to accommodate guests for whom he had no spare room, and there they could (in his words) be housed "quite snugly". He engaged the landlord, a man by the name of Trood (which might have suggested the name 'Drood'), to supply refreshments for the sporting events Dickens organised. Mr. Trood also did business on a more regular basis, as may be gleaned from the following anecdote told by F.G. Kitton about one of the waiters at the Sir John Falstaff:

> "A few days after Dickens' death, an Englishman, deeply grieved at the event, made a sort of pilgrimage to Gad's Hill. He went into the Sir John Falstaff and in the effusiveness of his honest emotion, could not avoid taking the waiter into his confidence.
> 'A great loss, this of Mr. Dickens,' he began.
> 'A very great loss to us, sir,' replied the waiter shaking his head, 'he had all his ale sent in from this house.'"

Relations between Dickens and the landlord were somewhat strained when Dickens first took possession. Dickens had not even learned the landlord's name correctly and addressed him as 'Mr. Strood', begging him "to be so good as to give directions that no rubbish or refuse from the Falstaff be thrown into the shrubbery of Gad's Hill Place", and hoping that "Mr. Strood will advise his customers not to trespass on that ground in going from the Falstaff to the village".

Relations subsequently became cordial, although there were times when the noise from the tavern was disturbing. One guest over Whitsuntide commented on the boisterous company across the way, and there was even more noise one summer's day in June 1859. As Dickens reported to his eldest daughter: "The Plorn [Master Edward Dickens, then aged 7] is highly excited today by reason of an institution which he tells me . . . is called the 'Cobb, or Bodderin', holding a festival at The Falstaff. He is possessed of some vague information that they go to Higham Church, in pursuance of some old usage, and attend service there, and afterwards march round the village. It so far looks probable that they certainly started off at eleven very spare in numbers, and came back considerably recruited, which looks to me like the difference between going to church and coming to dinner. They bore no end of bright banners and broad sashes, and had a band with a terrific drum, and are now (at half-past two) dining at the Falstaff, partly in the side room on the ground floor, and partly in a tent improvised this morning. The drum is hung up to a tree in The Falstaff garden, and looks like a tropical sort of gourd. I have presented the band with five shillings, which munificence has been highly appreciated. Ices don't seem to be provided for the ladies in the gallery* – I mean the garden; they are prowling about there endeavouring to peep in at the beef and mutton through the holes in the tent, on the whole, in a debased and degrading manner."

So much for the Old Dover Road and the tavern across the way: what about the house which Dickens came to buy? He referred to it as dating from Queen Anne's time, but in this he was mistaken. It was built in George III's reign, round about the year 1780, by a self-made man named Thomas Stephens who had begun his career as an ostler, later became a brewer, and eventually was elected Mayor of Rochester. He is reputed to have been barely literate, which perhaps accounts for the different spellings of his name – Stephens, Stevins, and Stevens – which occur in the records.

* Note: An allusion to the custom at grand public dinners in the Victorian age of the ladies listening to the speeches from the gallery, and being provided with ices.

Gad's Hill Place from the front lawn.

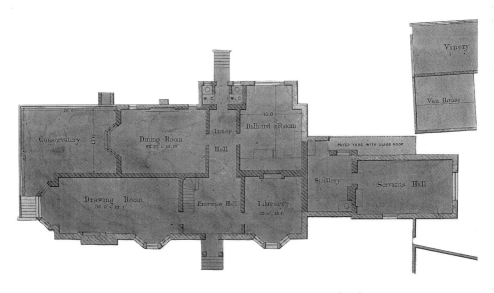

Plan of the ground floor of Gad's Hill Place, reproduced
from the plan issued by the auctioneer when the house was sold
following Dickens' death.

Opposite: A group on the steps of Gad's Hill Place – *standing*: Katey, Mamie, and Charles Dickens – *seated*: H. F. Chorley, Charles Collins (Katey's husband) and Georgina Hogarth.

Right and below: Two views of the library.

Above: W. H. Wills, Dickens' right-hand man in conducting *All the Year Round*. He learned that Gad's Hill Place belonged to Miss Eliza Lynn and that she wished to sell it.

Left: Dickens in the dress he often wore at Gad's Hill.

However, he had the good fortune to marry the daughter of a wealthy man, probably his employer, and this was possibly the key to his success, and his ability to build a substantial home for himself on Gad's Hill.

The building was known originally as Gad's Hill House, and after Thomas Stephens' death in 1806 was let to Messrs. Gunning, Berry, Comport and Gibbs, who seem to have leased it to the Maundrell family in 1818. The Maundrells apparently arrived as a newly-married couple, who during their tenancy produced a child every year (with one or two exceptions) until, by the time they left, they had a family of seven.

At some date the freehold passed to Sir Joseph Williamson's Mathematical School at Rochester, which continued in Dickens' time to own extensive land adjoining the Gad's Hill meadows to the South. In 1827 on the departure of the Maundrells the lease was acquired by the Reverend James Lynn, who in 1835 renewed it until 1840. This information can be gleaned from the tithe maps which began for this area in 1841 and list the landowners and occupiers of parish lands. The 1841 map reveals that by this date the freehold had been acquired by the Master and Fellows of St. John's College, Cambridge. Other sources of information are the decennial census returns, which from 1841 recorded the names of persons living in each house, and the ages of those over fifteen, expressed to the lower term of five. Thus only the approximate ages of those at Gad's Hill House on 6th June 1841 can be ascertained. The occupants, however, were as follows: James Thomas (20), his wife Fanny (30), Samuel Barnard (60), Caroline Phillips (20), and William Leonard (20). The last two, and possibly Samuel Barnard, were probably servants. What had become of Penelope Hulk who according to Piggot's Directory of 1840 was then occupying the house, is not recorded.

The 1851 census enquiry was more demanding. It asked for each person's exact age, place of birth, marital status, and relationship to the household. So the information concerning Gad's Hill House on 30th March 1851 was that it was occupied by the Vicar of Higham, the Rev. Joseph Hindle, aged 55, and his wife, Susanna, aged 49. Their 18-year-old daughter, Maria Elizabeth, and their 7-year-old son, David Brian, lived with them. There were also three guests in the house on that day – an unbeneficed clergyman, the Rev. Thomas Brocklebank, aged 63, and two spinsters, Miss Ann Ward, aged 29, and Miss Charlotte Elizabeth Ward, aged 25. Then there were three servants – Ann King,

aged 54, unmarried cook; Susanna Palmer, aged 23, housemaid; and
James Smead, aged 26, gardener.

The 1841 tithe map shows that Gad's Hill House had three
outhouses. The occupants of these in 1851 were Sarah Archer, aged 71,
the head of the household listed as 'Monthly Nurse' (and inevitably
bringing to mind that other monthly nurse, the immortal Sairey
Gamp); Richard Johnson, a farm labourer aged 24, head of a second
household, and his wife, Ann Johnson, aged 21. The third household
consisted of Robert Geal, a woodman aged 28, his wife, Jane, aged 29,
and their son George, aged 2.

It is not clear when the Rev. James Lynn acquired the freehold but it
was probably during the time he resided in the house. His younger
daughter, Eliza, was a rebellious girl, a freethinker, who later in her life
produced her own version of the gospel story, entitled *Joshua Davidson*.
She left home as soon as possible to embark on a journalistic career
which led her to London and Paris, and during the early years of her
career she wrote a number of unrealistic novels set in the Ancient
World. She also contributed to various journals, including *Household
Words*. W. H. Wills, the assistant editor of *Household Words*, evidently
did not realise she had any connection with the neighbourhood of
Higham until he met her at a dinner one evening in 1855. (Dickens,
however, seems to have been aware that at one time she had lived at the
Hermitage, the large house not far from Gad's Hill Place.) This evening,
Wills was appointed to escort Miss Lynn to dinner. In the course of
conversation he learned that she was well acquainted with the Higham
locality. "I was a child there." she told him, "in the house they call Gad's
Hill Place. My father was the rector, and lived there many years. He has
just died, has left it to me, and I want to sell it." Wills, who knew all
about Dickens having his eye on this particular property, went to
Dickens the next morning in great excitement. "It is written," he said,
"that you were to have that house at Gad's Hill. So you must buy it.
Now or never."

Said Dickens, recalling this incident: "I did".

CHAPTER 2

A Dream of My Childhood

Mention was made in the last chapter of the fanciful episode in one of the *Uncommercial Traveller* essays in which Dickens met the 'very queer small boy' (himself) on the road to Gad's Hill. Their imaginary conversation did not merely concern Falstaff, however: the very queer small boy was keenly interested in the house at the top of the hill and wanted the carriage halted so that he might stare at it "out of window".

> " 'You admire that house?' said I.
> 'Bless you, sir,' said the very queer small boy, 'when I was not more than half as old as nine, it used to be a treat for me to be brought to look at it. And now, I am nine, I come by myself to look at it. And ever since I can recollect, my father, seeing me so fond of it, has often said to me, 'If you were to be very persevering and were to work hard, you might some day come to live in it.' Though that's impossible!' "

Although his father's prophecy seemed impossible, thoughts of the house were never far from Dickens' mind. In 1843, while in 'agonies' of 'blazing away' at *Chuzzlewit* and *A Christmas Carol* simultaneously, he undoubtedly recalled it when he described the Spirit of Christmas Past taking Scrooge to the scenes of his childhood. The 'solitary child', whom they encountered neglected by his friends, was another manifestation of the 'very queer small boy'. Not surprisingly therefore the scene in Dickens' mind was set on Gad's Hill, so Scrooge and the Spirit "left the high-road by a well-remembered lane, and soon approached a mansion of dull red brick, with a little weathercock-surmounted cupola on the roof, and a bell hanging in it."

Yet the dream was not impossible. On Dickens' 43rd birthday, 7th February 1855, he saw a notice on the property: "For sale".

He had been down to Gravesend that day. It was bitterly cold weather and the snow lay thick on the ground. Fortunately the road had been cleared and the snow piled up along the side in walls varying between three and six feet high. Otherwise he could not have walked down to Rochester. When he saw the sale notice, he could hardly believe his eyes, and hastened to get in touch with the agent. The owner of the freehold, the Rev. James Lynn, had died as recently as 1st February, and no time had been lost in putting the house on the market, although it was still occupied by the leaseholder, the Rev. Joseph Hindle.

Dickens does not seem to have known that the vendor was one of his contributors to *Household Words*, nor that as a child she had lived in the house. But he did know that she was familiar with the locality, because on 9th February he wrote to Wills: "When I was at Gravesend t'other day, I saw, at Gad's Hill – just opposite to the Hermitage, where your charmer Miss Lynn used to live – a little freehold to be sold. The spot and the very house are literally 'a dream of my childhood', and I should like to look at it before I go to Paris. With that purpose I must go to Strood by the North Kent, at a quarter-past ten tomorrow morning, and I want you, strongly booted, to go with me. (I know the particulars from the agent.)"

It seems that the oft-repeated story that Dickens first heard from Wills about the availability of Gad's Hill Place is not strictly true. He himself discovered it was for sale, but Wills evidently supplied the information that its owner was Miss Lynn who was anxious to sell. The story about Wills at the dinner party was contained in a letter from Dickens to De Cerjat nearly two years later, and cannot be regarded as entirely accurate.

Dickens was fortunate in having as his brother-in-law a highly competent architect and engineer, Henry Austin. The two men had been intimate friends from their early twenties, and Austin had married Dickens' younger sister, Letitia. He had prospered in his career and gained some distinction. Not surprisingly, when Dickens needed professional help and advice he went to Henry. Already, on acquiring the lease of Tavistock House, and wishing to make numerous alterations he had found Henry a very useful man. Austin had gone over the whole property, examining it in great detail, preparing plans for the work required, and drawing up an estimate of the cost. Recollecting the infinite trouble Austin had gone to on that occasion his grateful brother-in-law now called him in to have a look at the state of Gad's Hill Place.

Austin was happy to oblige and came along to inspect the foundations, walls, roof, drainage and water-supply. Dickens later informed his friend, Miss Coutts: "Mr. Austin surveyed it for me, and was greatly struck by it. Large sums of money have been expended on it (for such a small place) at various times, and he found everything about the garden and so forth, in the best order. There is a very pretty garden, and shrubbery on the other side of the high road, at which the house looks. When I exhibit it to you with all my contrivances accomplished – of course some of them will be wonderfully ingenious – I will tell you what I paid for it."

His bargaining over the price added to the time it took to complete the purchase. Dickens had appointed Wills to conduct the negotiations on his behalf, but he felt that Miss Lynn was asking more than the property was worth. She wanted £2,000, but Henry Austin advised that £1,700 was enough. Evidently, Wills reported to Dickens that Miss Lynn was determined to get her price and was not budging. So Dickens wrote to instruct him: "I too would like to try the effect of 'not budging'. So do not go beyond the £1,700. Considering what I should have to expend on the one hand, the low price of stock on the other, I do not feel disposed to go beyond that mark. They won't let a purchaser escape for the sake of £100, I think."

There was in fact considerable bargaining, and at one stage Dickens even advised Wills to withdraw if the agents for the other side refused to accept his offer. In the end, however, he agreed to pay a slightly higher price than Austin had suggested, and a deal was made. Miss Lynn (who became Mrs. Lynn Linton in 1858) recorded later in *My Literary Life*: "We sold it cheap – £1,700 – and we asked £40 for the ornamental timber. To this Dickens and his agent made an objection, so we had an arbitrator who awarded us £70, which was in the nature of a triumph." The legal business was conducted by his solicitor, Frederic Ouvry, and eventually on 14th March 1856, Dickens was able to inform his sister-in-law, Georgina Hogarth: "This day I have paid the purchase-money for Gad's Hill Place. After drawing the cheque, I turned round to give it to Wills, and said: 'Now isn't it an extraordinary thing – look at the day – Friday! I have been nearly drawing it half-a-dozen times, when the lawyers have not been ready, and here it comes round upon a Friday, as a matter of course.'" He had been born on a Friday, had moved into his present home, Tavistock House on a Friday, and believed that all the important events in his life tended to happen, by accident, on a Friday.

Dickens was very careful over money matters. He was always to worry greatly over the expenses involved in running Gad's Hill, even complaining at times about the cost of small items such as plants for the garden. So when it came to find such a large sum as £1,770 he hesitated before selling any stock. He knew the market was depressed, and he would probably sell at a loss. So he turned to his publishers, Bradbury and Evans to say, first of all, "that if it should be convenient to you even to increase upon the £200 monthly payment, it will suit me perfectly well", and then to add "And be so good as to make up the last half-year's account with as little delay as you can, because, having this purchase to make I am glad just now of all the money I can get. I know that the usual time has not yet arrived, but you may perhaps be able to anticipate it a little, knowing my desire."

Having acquired the freehold of the property, Dickens found that much needed to be done to it. He wrote to Forster on 9th February 1856, while the final legal matters had still to be settled: "The changes absolutely necessary will take a thousand pounds; which sum I am always resolving to squeeze out of this, grind out of that, and wring out of the other; this, that, and the other generally all three declining to come up to the scratch for the purpose."

It was with the expenses of Gad's Hill in mind that a year or two later he was to suggest reviving an idea which he had put forward tentatively once or twice already – that he should give public readings from his books and thereby have a second source of income.

Dickens could not take possession of his new property immediately because the Rector of Higham, the Rev. Joseph Hindle, was still living there. In fact, "the good old Rector" (as Dickens called him) had been in the house for twenty-six years and his lease did not expire until Lady Day 1857. As Dickens explained to Miss Coutts:

". . . the object Wills and I have in view in going down there directly, is to ask him how and when it will suit his convenience to come out – as of course I wish to treat him with all handsome consideration. It is not now a furnished house, but my object is, as soon as I have got rid of the tenant, to make it clean and pretty in the papering and painting way, and then to furnish it in the most comfortable and cosey [sic] manner, and let it by the month whenever I can. Whenever I cannot, I shall use it for myself and make it a change for Charley from Saturday to Monday. When all this is done, I shall have a delight in taking you down to see it which I shall not try here to express; and if you should like it so well as to think of ever occupying it as a little easy change, I shall be far more attached to the spot than ever. I think you will be very much pleased with it. It is so old-fashioned, plain, and comfortable. On the summit of Gad's Hill, with a noble prospect at the side and behind, looking down into the Valley of the Medway. Lord Darnley's Park at Cobham (a beautiful place with a noble walk through a wood) is close by it; and Rochester is within a mile or two. It is only an hour and a quarter from London by the Railway. To crown all, the sign of the Sir John Falstaff is over the way, and I used to look at it as a wonderful Mansion (which God knows it is not), when I was a very odd child with the first faint shadows of all my books in my head – I suppose."

The Rev. Mr. Hindle stayed on until March 1857, and Dickens then set about preparing Gad's Hill Place for his own occupation. There was a great deal to be done. Workmen came in, and Dickens took his wife and sister-in-law to Waite's Hotel at Gravesend so that he could supervise the various alterations and the "ingenious devices" he had promised would be a feature of the house.

A house-warming party was arranged for Tuesday, 19th May, and Dickens sent precise details to the friends he was inviting. To Wilkie Collins (who, Dickens perhaps suspected, did not understand the new mode of expressing railway time) he wrote: "The train which will bring down the main body of the small army who inaugurate Gad's Hill Place with cold meat next Tuesday, leaves London Bridge Station at 3.40 – twenty minutes before 4. Take return for Gravesend. Put yourself under the guidance of the gallant Wills, and he will lead you to Victory." He wrote in similar terms to Thomas Beard, but as Beard had proposed to stay a whole day in the country, Dickens suggested he should remain on the train until it reached Higham. There, provided Beard notified his host of his intended time of arrival, Dickens ("the Inimitable Kentish Freeholder") would be at the station to meet him. There were as yet neither horses nor carriages at Gad's Hill, so Beard was warned that he would have "to walk a mile to my Numble abode". This was the first of many arrangements to meet guests and bring them up from Higham station.

That summer the Dickens family moved into their new home – not permanently, for Dickens had no intention at this stage of giving up Tavistock House. Gad's Hill was to be a summer residence only, or, if the family were away, it was to be let. Some years later, Dickens did arrange to exchange houses for some months with a friend. This enabled him to have a London house for the London season. But he never actually let it by the month as he had originally intended.

So, with the house-warming satisfactorily performed, he explained to his friend, the Rev. James White:

"We purpose going to Gad's Hill for the summer on the First of June; as, apart from the master's eye being a necessary ornament to the spot, I clearly see that the workmen yet lingering in the yard must be squeezed out by bodily pressure, or they will never go."

Even before the place was occupied, Dickens began to throw out invitations to his friends. The Rev. White and his family were told, "we can take you all in, on your way north". Arthur Smith and his brother Albert were asked to fix a Sunday for coming down "to see me in a little house I have on the identical spot where Falstaff ran away when they set upon the travellers – most appropriate ground for being jovial on." Miss Coutts was told: "After the first of June, I shall be inconsolable until I have fairly laid hold of you and Mrs. Brown and taken you in captivity down to Gad's Hill." And he had already agreed to accommodate Hans Christian Andersen "(who has been 'coming' for about three years)" during what Dickens expected to be a fort-night's stay in England.

The actual move was not accomplished without some incidental chaos. Dickens wrote to Wilkie Collins:

"In consequence of bedevilment at Gad's Hill, arising from the luggage wandering over the face of the earth, I shall have to pass tomorrow behind a hedge, attired in leaves from my own fig-tree. . . . When last heard of, the family itself (including the birds and the goldfinch on his perch) had been swept away from the stupefied John by a crowd of Whitsun holiday-makers, and had gone (without tickets) somewhere down into Sussex. A desperate calmness has fallen upon me. I don't care."

The family at this time (1857) consisted of Mrs. Catherine Dickens, her sister Georgina Hogarth, the two Dickens girls – Mamie (19) and Katey (18), and the seven Dickens boys – Charley (20), Walter (16), Frank (13), Alfred (12), Sydney (10), Harry (8), and Edward (known as Plorn) (4). Charley had been away from home while he was at Eton College, and again while he was in Germany, but he was now, for a short while, back with the family. Walter had been at Wimbledon, preparing to take up a Cadetship in the East India Company's 26th Native Infantry, and was to sail for India within two months of the occupation of Gad's Hill. Frank, Alfred and Sydney were still at school in Boulogne. So all the family was at Gad's Hill Place for a mere matter of weeks. By the time of Dickens' death, the members residing there permanently would be reduced to two – Georgina and Mamie. They had not been there a few days, however, when they were faced with a serious crisis. The well had run dry. They had pumped out only sufficient water to supply the family's needs for a day, and no more was available. The following day there was hardly any again. Dickens lost no time in getting in touch with Henry Austin and seeking his help.

"It is pretty clear to me," he wrote, "that we must look the thing in the face, and at once bore deeper, dig, or do some beastly thing or other, to secure this necessary in abundance. Meanwhile I am in a most plaintive and forlorn condition without your presence and council. I raise my voice in the wilderness and implore the same!!! Wild legends are in circulation among the servants how that Captain Goldsmith on the knoll above – the skipper in that crow's-nest of a house – has millions of gallons of water always flowing for him. Can he have damaged my well? Can we imitate him, and have one millions of gallons? Goldsmith or I must fall, so I conceive."

Providing a reliable water supply was to be one of the most costly undertakings in the new property. Eventually a new well was drilled to a depth of 217 feet. The water was pumped out by means of a horse-driven pump and held in a cistern on the roof of the house. This was a daily job, and took the horse 20 minutes, walking round and round in the pumping-room, to draw sufficient water for the day's needs.

But before this satisfactory solution had been reached, Dickens had to endure months of anguish as workmen came and went, and expenses mounted while the work seemed to make little progress. "We are still boring for water here," he wrote to Forster, "at the rate of two pounds per day for wages. The men seem to like it very much, and to be perfectly comfortable. . . ."

Then suddenly, in August, there was water – and enough! Dickens at once dashed off an urgent note to Henry Austin:

"At last, I am happy to inform you, we have got at a famous spring!! It rushed in this morning, ten foot deep. And our friends talk of its supplying 'a ton a minute for yourself and your family, sir, for evermore.' They ask leave to bore ten feet lower, to prevent the possibility of what they call 'a choking with sullage'. Likewise, they are going to insert 'a rose-headed pipe'; at the mention of which implement, I am (secretly) well-nigh distracted, having no idea of what it means. But I have said 'Yes', besides instantly standing a bottle of gin.

Can you come back, and can you get down on Monday morning, to
advise and endeavour to decide on the mechanical force we shall use for
raising the water?"

Later letters told of the progress (or lack of it) in getting the pumping
machinery into operation:

"Here are six men perpetually going up and down the well (I know
somebody will be killed), in the course of fitting a pump; which is quite
a railway terminus – it is so iron, and so big. The process is much more
like putting Oxford Street endwise and laying gas along it, than
anything else. By the time it is finished, the cost of this water will be
something absolutely frightful. But of course it proportionately
increases the value of the property, and that's my only comfort." And
the work continued to drag on. "Five men have been looking attentively
at the pump for a week, and (I should hope) may begin to fit it in the
course of October."

There was also trouble with the drains. Two new cess-pools had to be
created, and this entailed digging up the flower-beds to lay new drain-
pipes. The garden was therefore a muddy swamp, trampled over by
irresponsible labourers. So, between drainage contractors and well-
borers, Dickens was driven nearly frantic in his first few months of
occupancy.

A minor matter for concern was a marauding cat which seemed
determined to get at the family's pet birds. Dickens was even more
concerned over the drastic measures being adopted by his servant,
French, to deal with the menace. He wrote to Forster in July:

"About four pounds of powder and half a ton of shot have been fired
off at the cat (and the public in general) during the week. The finest
thing is that immediately after I have heard the noble sportsman blazing
away at her in the garden in front, I look out of my room door into the
drawing-room, and am pretty sure to see her coming in after the birds,
in the calmest manner, by the back window. Intelligence had been
brought to me from a source on which I can rely, that French has newly
conceived the atrocious project of tempting her into the coach-house by
meat and kindness, and there, from an elevated portmanteau, blowing
her head off. This I mean sternly to interdict, and to do so today as a
work of piety."

Another thing which troubled Dickens as the summer wore on and
the time came round for the annual hop-picking, was the condition of
many of the poor folk who came down for this seasonal employment.

"Hop-picking is going on," he told Forster, "and people sleep in the garden, and breathe in at the keyhole of the house door. I have been amazed, before this year, by the number of miserable lean wretches, hardly able to crawl, who go hop-picking. I find it is a superstition, that the dust of the newly-picked hop, falling freshly into the throat, is a cure for consumption. So the poor creatures drag themselves along the roads, and sleep under wet hedges, and get cured soon and finally."

On 19th July, the first break-up of the Gad's Hill family took place. Dickens accompanied by his eldest son, Charley, went down to Southampton to say good-bye to his second son, Walter, who was sailing to India to join his regiment. It was a sad parting. Seeing his two sons going aboard the ship ahead of him, Dickens felt he was looking at photographs of his own back at sixteen and twenty. Bidding farewell was like having "great teeth drawn with a wrench", and the next day, when he was lying on the grass at Gad's Hill in a reflective mood, Dickens wondered "whether the last definition of man may not be, after all, that he is (for his sins) a parting and farewell-taking animal". He was never to see Walter again. The "poor fellow" who had "steamed away yesterday", died at Calcutta on 31st December 1863.

Thus Dickens acquired Gad's Hill Place and spent his first summer there. By the end of that summer his life was beginning to change. Indeed, the day when he walked between the walls of snow from Gravesend to Rochester and saw the notice "For Sale" on the house which had been "the dream of his childhood", was to prove the watershed in his life.

On that day he had been the tenant of Tavistock House and must have fully expected to remain there indefinitely. He was a married man with nine children, some temporarily away, but all usually coming home to spend the summer holidays or enjoy the Christmas festivities. He had written to De Cerjat at the beginning of that year: "The whole nine are well and happy. Ditto, Mrs. Dickens, Ditto, Georgina." And letters to his wife still began "My dearest Catherine" and concluded "Yours affectionately".

On that day he was the editor of *Household Words* and there seemed no reason why he should not continue to occupy the editorial chair indefinitely. He was on good terms with his publishers, Bradbury and Evans. His son Charley was courting Bessie Evans, the publisher's daughter, and there seemed no impediment to their being married in due course with the approval of all concerned. On 6th February (the day before he went on his snowy walk) he perceived "motes of new stories floating before my eyes in the dirty air", and from this vague beginning *Little Dorrit* was to develop, the last twenty-part novel for another nine years. In fact, his rate of novel-writing was to slow down drastically. In the nine years between 1846 and the end of 1854, he had written three major novels – *Dombey and Son*, *David Copperfield*, and *Bleak House* and a shorter one, *Hard Times*. After the last part of *Little Dorrit* was published, which coincided with the Dickens family moving to Gad's Hill, he was to produce, in the thirteen years left to him, two shorter novels – *A Tale of Two Cities* and *Great Expectations*; one major novel – *Our Mutual Friend*, and six parts of *Edwin Drood*.

His appearance was also to undergo a change. Until 1850 he had been generally clean-shaven, although he had grown a beard for theatrical productions, subsequently shaving it off, and from time to time had sported a moustache. When he sat for the portrait by Ary Schaffer in November 1855, he had quite a small beard. This had grown into a much fuller one by January 1859 when he sat for Frith. His friends and family had thought the earlier moustache 'a hideous disfigurement', and sittings to Frith were delayed in the hope that he would soon be as clean-shaven as he had appeared in Mayall's photograph of 1849. Beards were fashionable, however, in honour of the heroes of the Crimean War, and Dickens refused to bow to his family's wishes. From about the time when he made his walk from Gravesend, he was permanently bearded. The youthful Boz gave way to the prematurely old Uncommercial Traveller.

The greatest change was, unhappily, in his private life. On the evening of 9th February after he had told Wills of the house being for sale, and asked him to go down with him to view it, something happened which was to unbalance him, and disturb the entire tenor of his life. The next day he wrote:

"As I was reading by my fire last night, a handful of notes was laid down on my table. I looked them over, and, recognising the writing of no private friend, let them lie there and went back to my book. But I found my mind curiously disturbed, and wandering away through so many years to such early times of my life, that I was quite perplexed to account for it. . . . At last it came into my head that it must have been suggested by something in the look of one of those letters. So I turned them over again – and suddenly the remembrance of your hand came upon me with an influence that I cannot express to you." The letter was from Maria Beadnell (now Mrs. Winter) the girl he had been so deeply in love with as a youth of nineteen and twenty. "Three or four and twenty years vanished like a dream, and I opened it with the touch of my young friend David Copperfield when he was in love."

The old feelings stirred again in Dickens' breast, even though when he met Maria again (in a surreptitious way), she proved to be a great disappointment. Maria "whom he had left a lily, had become a peony". The woman "who had been spoiled and artless long ago, was determined to be spoiled and artless now". Nevertheless, she had aroused feelings by reminding him of his youthful passion, which could not be suppressed. His dissatisfaction with Catherine, which had been muted and hidden, now began to poison his mind. His restlessness became accentuated. His unhappiness increased.

Then on 9th June 1857 (a significant date) Dickens was travelling up to London by train from Higham. With him were Catherine and Georgina. A man in the same carriage took out his newspaper, unfolded it, glanced down at the news and remarked to his companion: "I see that Douglas Jerrold is dead." Dickens overheard, and the intelligence deeply shocked him. Ten days earlier Dickens had dined with Jerrold at Greenwich but had no idea how ill Jerrold had been in the meantime. He at once resolved to raise money for the Jerrold family and to do so he set about organising various fund-raising events. He himself would give public readings, but the main event would be the revival of Wilkie Collins' play *The Frozen Deep* which Dickens and his amateur company had presented at Tavistock House earlier in the year. This revival was a great success. A special performance was put on for the benefit of the Queen at the Gallery of Illustration in Regent Street. In August it was decided to give performances at the Manchester Free Trade Hall. This was a very large hall and because it was feared that the amateur actresses would be unable to make themselves heard, Dickens decided to engage professionals. These were the Ternans – Mrs. Frances Ternan and her daughters, Maria and Ellen. In this way Dickens became acquainted with Ellen with whom he fell secretly but disquieteningly in love. Two months had passed since the family had moved into Gad's Hill.

Things went from bad to worse. Dickens confided in his friend, Forster, about the strains in his married life, but did not find much comfort in Forster's reply. "To the most part of what you say – Amen!" he wrote. "You are not so tolerant as perhaps you might be of the wayward and unsettled feeling which is part (I suppose) of the tenure on which one holds an imaginative life." The home atmosphere became unbearable – at least for the adults; the younger children probably knew nothing of what was going on. In September, Dickens went on a tour of Cumberland and North Yorkshire with Wilkie Collins, and on his return to Gad's Hill gave detailed instructions to his old servant, Anne Cornelius, to have alterations made to the bedroom at Tavistock House. These ensured that from then on, Dickens and his wife would have separate sleeping-quarters. Nor after several stormy scenes did he continue to reside with her. Catherine's mother and father came to stay at Tavistock House, and (although her father, George Hogarth, had been a colleague of his during his years on *The Morning Post*) Dickens had developed an intense dislike for them. He declared he could not "bear the contemplation of their imbecility any more", and one evening when matters came to a head he left Tavistock House and set off to walk to Gad's Hill, thirty miles away, arriving there the next morning.

Finally, Dickens and Catherine separated. She went to live at 70 Gloucester Crescent, Regent's Park, and the eldest son, Charley, went to live with her. So the family was reduced by a further two in April 1858.

The separation was not effected without a great deal of trouble all round. Dickens' younger daughter, Katey, said later: "My father was like a madman when my mother left home. This affair brought out all that was worst, all that was weakest in him." He certainly quarrelled with many of his old friends. He broke with Mark Lemon, editor of *Punch*, over his refusal to publish a statement about the separation. He broke with the proprietors of *Punch*, Bradbury and Evans, and because they were also proprietors of *Household Words*, he gave up editing that journal and founded a new one called *All the Year Round*. He had to find new publishers for his novels, and therefore went back to Chapman and Hall, the firm which had published *Pickwick* and his early books.

The other great change in his life-style resulted from the decision to engage in public readings from his works. The heavy expenditure on the property no doubt inclined his thoughts in this direction, but Dickens loved the direct contact with an audience which the readings gave him. He read several times for the Douglas Jerrold Fund, which made him continually yearn for the applause and immediate adulation which readings afforded. But they were to ruin his health, and took him away from his desk for long periods. So the incidence of novels began to decline. He was to some extent compelled to write the next two – *A Tale of Two Cities* was needed to launch the new *All the Year Round*, and *Great Expectations* was an essential prop to restore falling sales after disappointment over Charles Lever's serial *A Day's Ride: A Life's Romance*. Admittedly, he had ideas for these works roaming about in his mind before the imperative need for them arose, but they might have assumed different forms and been written later if there had not been these pressures. Eventually, readings were to make the first call on Dickens' time and energy.

CHAPTER 3

Gad's Hill Place – The House and Grounds

There are a number of descriptions of Gad's Hill Place, which, together with the sale catalogue, numerous photographs and a knowledge of many of the surviving contents of the house, enable a reasonably good idea to be obtained of what it was like when Dickens lived there.

It stood at the summit of Gad's Hill, just opposite the entrance to the road leading down to Higham railway station. In the angle formed by this road and the main high road, was the shrubbery (or "Wilderness" as Dickens called it) where he erected his chalet. The principal features of this Wilderness, and its crowning glory, were two immense cedars which unfortunately were so weakened by storms in 1907 that they had to be felled. It was reckoned they were then 121 years old. The Wilderness was reached from the house by a tunnel beneath the road. This, which still exists, was constructed by Dickens' brother, Alfred, and has so far withstood all the pounding of traffic which has passed overhead during the last century and more.

The house was surrounded by a substantial wall; access from the road to the semi-circular drive was gained through either of two sets of tall wooden gates hung from stone gate-posts. The gravel drive enclosed the front lawn from which steps descended into the tunnel. Laurel bushes and a bed of scarlet geraniums filled the strip of garden between the house and the drive. On either side of the entrance was a variegated holly bush.

Stone steps led up to the front door. These were sheltered by a small pillared portico, and behind each pillar was a wooden seat for summer-time idlers. (The wood was reputedly from furniture which had once belonged to Shakespeare.) A large ornate lantern hung from the angle of the portico-roof to light the steps at night-time.

Entering the house, visitors found themselves in a large square hall with a parquet floor leading to a passage with a door at the far end giving access to the rear garden. On the wall to the right were the backdrops for the plays *The Lighthouse* and *The Frozen Deep* which had been painted by Clarkson Stanfield. The first door on the right led into Dickens' library, and the second door into the billiard room. On the left was the door to the drawing room, and the broad staircase going to the next floor. Both sides of the panels of the balustrade had been painted with designs by Katey. Another door on the left led downstairs to the kitchen and other domestic offices, and beyond this was the entrance to the dining-room. Adjacent to this was a dumb waiter, or serving lift, which brought up trays, etc. from the kitchen below. At either side of the narrow passage which led from the inner hall to the steps leading to the rear garden was a lavatory.

The accommodation on the upper floors, according to the advertisement announcing the sale of the property after Dickens' death, consisted of four good bedrooms on the first floor, one with enclosure to form a dressing room, a bathroom, WC, and staircase leading to two bachelors' bedrooms. On the upper floor were two large bedrooms with enclosures to form dressing-rooms, two bedrooms for servants, and a spacious landing. The basement consisted of a large servants' hall and scullery (which were both situated to the right of the library and billiard room), a kitchen, butler's pantry, larder, china closet, large wine, beer, and coal cellars, a WC and a small paved yard with glass roof to the rear of the servants' hall. Gas was laid on.

Dickens made a number of improvements to the building, some of which have led to serious difficulties for subsequent occupiers. He extended the drawing room by removing the wall and fireplace which faced the entrance. There must have been a window also in this wall, because Dickens had observed the cat being hunted by French "coming in . . . by the back window". He extended the frontage of the house by building a new outside wall in which was set the new fireplace and chimney, extended the inner wall, and built a new rear wall with window. By doing this, he removed the principal support of the chimney breast in the upper storeys. The beam, inserted under the ceiling where the wall had been, has unfortunately bowed under the weight above as the years have gone by and allowed damp to penetrate. Two girders also had to be put in place, as Dickens reported to Wilkie Collins on 24th September 1863:

"The girders were both got up by 8 o'clock at night. It was ticklish work – nine men gasping, snuffling, heaving, snorting, balancing themselves on bricks, and tumbling over each other. But it really was well done, and with great cheerfulness and spirit, to which three gallons of beer, judiciously thrown in, imparted a festive air. Nothing has fallen down or blown up since. Yawning chasms abound, and dust obscures all objects; but we hope to weather it."

The extension of the drawing-room permitted Dickens to build a conservatory which in effect was a very similar extension to the adjoining dining-room. This was constructed of iron pillars, with windows between, each window having a semi-circle of glass in the upper light. The conservatory had a glass roof, and a tiled floor, and was heated from a boiler-house below. The catalogue of the sale of furniture, etc. reveals that Dickens had the conservatory extremely well filled with a variety of plants, and we know that just before his death he was busy hanging up Chinese lanterns therein. It must have been a delightful place – warm, heavy with the scent of flowers, and at night-time romantically lit. Dickens was particularly proud of this "positively the last improvement to Gad's Hill," as he told his daughter. Forster recorded "This last addition had long been an object of desire with him, though he would hardly . . . have given himself the indulgence but for the golden shower from America. He saw it first in a completed state on the Sunday before his death, when his youngest daughter was on a visit to him."

The other important structural improvement was the alteration of the attic storey to permit the use of it as bedrooms. This and other work was carried out by Mr. J. Couchman, a Strood building contractor. Specifications for this work, drawn up on 20th September 1861, were as follows:

> "*Bricklayer*: To take off slates and coping and heighten brick walls and chimneys, and build No. 2 new chimneys with stock and picking bricks laid in cement. No. 2 chimney bars to cope gable ends with old stone. No. 2 hearthstones. No. 2 plain stone chimney-pieces. No. 2–2 ft. 6 in. Register stoves. To lath and plaster ceiling, side walls, and partitions with lime and hair two coats, and set to slate the new roof with good countess slates and metal nails. *Carpenter*: To take off roof, to lay floor joist with 7 × 2½ in. yellow battens; to fix roof, ceiling, joist and partitions of good fir timber, 4 ft. × 2 ft.; to use old timber that is sound and fit for use; to close

board roof, lead flat and gutters; to lay 1 in. × 9 in. white deal
floors, to skirt rooms with 8 in. × $\frac{3}{4}$ in. deal; to fix No. 4 pairs
of 1$\frac{3}{4}$ in. sashes and frames for plate-glass as per order. *All the
sashes to have weights and pulleys for opening.* To fix No. 2–6 ft. 6
in. × 2 ft. 6 in. 1$\frac{1}{2}$ in., four panel doors, and encase frames
with all necessary mouldings; to fix window linings, and 1$\frac{1}{2}$
in. square framings and doors for No. 2 dressing-rooms; to
fix No. 2, 7 in. rim locks, No. 2 box latches, sash fastenings,
sash weights, to fix 4 in. O.G. iron eaves, gutter with cistern
heads, and 3 in. iron leading pipes. *Plumber, Glazier, and
Painter*: To take up old lead guttering, and lay new gutters
and lead flats with 6 lb lead, ridge and flushings with 5 lb
lead; to paint all wood and iron-work that requires painting
4 coats in oil, the windows to be glazed with good plate glass;
to paper rooms and landings when walls are dry with paper
of the value of 1s 6d per piece, the old lead to be the property
of the plumber. *The two cisterns to be carried up and replaced on
new roof, the pipes attached to them to be lengthened as required by
the alterations; and a water-tap to be fitted in each dressing-room.*
All old materials not used and rubbish to be carted away by
the contractor. All the work to be completed in a sound and
workmanlike manner to the satisfaction of C. Dickens, Esq.,
for the sum of £241. The roof to be slated and flat covered
with lead in one month from commencing the work. The
whole to be completed – paper excepted – and all rubbish
cleared away by the 30th day of November, 1861."

For some of the time while all this work was being undertaken Dickens
was away on his second series of readings in the provinces. So Georgina
and Mamie had to deal with the workmen, and put up with the
inconvenience. On the 25th November, Dickens was in Berwick, but
not unmindful that Mr. Couchman's deadline was drawing near. "I
shall hope to hear very soon that the workmen have 'broken through'",
he wrote to Georgina, "and that you have been in the state apartments,
and that upholstery measurements have come off."

These, together with the well and pump already described, were the
major improvements to the house, although the tunnel beneath the
road was almost as great an enterprise. The fitting of the library door
with its dummy book-backs was a much simpler job, and one which, by

amusing generations of visitors, has amply repaid the effort on it. Dickens had probably borrowed the idea from the Duke of Devonshire's residence at Chatsworth, and had installed a similar door at Tavistock House. Some of the book-backs were repeated at Gad's Hill: *Hansard's Guide to Refreshing Sleep; Cat's Lives, 9 vols.; The Quarrelly Review, 4 vols.; History of a Short Chancery Suit, 21 vols.; The Wisdom of our Ancestors – I. Ignorance. II. Superstition. III. The Block. IV. The Stake. V. The Rack. VI. Dirt. VII. Disease.*

Another improvement was the tiling of the billiard-room walls to prevent damage from players' cues. Indeed, Dickens was justified in believing that anyone who had seen the house when he first bought it would have been astonished to see it in his later years.

There were many interesting things to be seen in and around the house. In the hall, besides the backdrops by Stanfield, there was a barometer and thermometer, a little statue of Diana, a plaster bust of Serjeant Talfourd, the jaws of a shark presented to him by Lieutenant Andrew Gordon, R.N. (a young man who sought to be Katey Dickens' suitor), the original of Grip, the raven, now stuffed and in a glass case, and a horseshoe. The most important item, however, was a large 8-day chiming clock in a beautifully carved wooden case, made by Bennett of Cheapside. On 14th September 1863 Dickens had to complain to the clockmaker in the following terms:

"My Dear Sir, – Since my hall clock was sent to your establishment to be cleaned it has gone (as indeed it always has) perfectly well, but has struck the hours with great reluctance, and after enduring internal agonies of a most distressing nature, it has now ceased striking altogether. Though a happy release for the clock, this is not convenient to the household. If you can send down any confidential person to whom the clock can confer, I think it may have something on its works that it would be glad to make a clean breast of – Faithfully yours, Charles Dickens."

In Dickens' library, or study, besides the door disguised as a bookcase, there was the desk and chair made familiar by Sir Luke Fildes' drawing of *The Empty Chair*. On top of the desk were the various objects Dickens enjoyed having in front of him when he was writing – the two fat toads fencing, the little monkey wearing a pill-box cap, the statuette of a dog-fancier with little dogs under his arms and peeping out of his pockets, the gilt leaf on which a rabbit was sitting erect. He also had a little box for holding string, a spring-balance for weighing letters, and a perpetual calendar. In this room, too, was the plaster cast of an Ottoman Turk wearing a fez, baggy trousers, and curly-toed shoes, seated comfortably on a divan enjoying a smoke from a hookah. Dickens himself explained its provenance: "I bought at Boulogne a little figure for my study chimney-piece which was the sign of a tobacconist's shop, and which, for the most grotesque absurdity, I consider un-rivalled."

The library was lined with bookshelves indistinguishable from the mock bookshelves in the door. An embossed leather pelmet depended from the edge of each shelf to protect the tops of the books below from dust. Many of the books were presentation copies such as Leigh Hunt's *Poetical Works* inscribed "To Charles Dickens from his constant admirer and obliged friend. Leigh Hunt. 1844." Talfourd's *Ion* and *The Athenian Captive* (which were bound together in one volume) contained a sonnet to Dickens on the flyleaf – "On Perusing the completed *Oliver Twist*, Christmas Day 1838." Another of Talfourd's works – *Recollections of a First Visit to the Alps in August and September 1841* – had called forth a comment from Dickens when he saw the dedication to "HER" that it was "rather Adam-and-Evey". The books provided some indication of Dickens' preferred reading. He enjoyed books of exploration and travel, such as Dr. Mavor's *Voyages and Travels from the Discovery of America to the Nineteenth Century* and Thomasina Ross's translation of Von Tshudi's *Travels in Peru during the Years 1838–42*. Perhaps his favourite of such works was W.H. Prescott's *The History of the Conquest of Mexico*, concerning which, Dickens said: "I am full of delight and pleasure – dreaming of it, talking of it, and thinking of it."

There were several books which revealed Dickens' interest in magic, apparitions, the medical aspects of death, premature interments, and the incubation of insanity. Others were books he had used for background information for his own writings: Vincent's pamphlet *A plain and succinct narration of the late Riots and Disturbances, With an Account of the Commitment of Lord George Gordon to the Tower*, and Theodore D. Weld's anti-slavery pamphlet which Dickens quoted in his chapter on slavery in *American Notes*.

The ones which he read most frequently were perhaps the volumes of State trials, Old Bailey trials, etc., the ten volumes of Ballantyne's Novelists Library (Smollett, Fielding, and Sterne) concerning which he declared that no-one had read them younger than he. Although only a new copy of William Cullan Bryant's *Poems* was found in the library on his death, the first copy according to Dickens had been so well-thumbed that no lettering appeared on its cover except one gilt 'B', and the remotest possible traces of a 'y'. Tennyson's *Poems* were also frequently taken off the shelf, and Dickens' copy bore numerous pencil marks. But amongst his greatest favourites were the now forgotten novels of Paul de Koch, several of which were to be found on his shelves.

On the opposite side of the hall was the drawing-room, which, as already noted, was extended to double its original length. At some stage, the chimney-piece which had been in this room in 1861 was moved to the billiard room, where it has remained, though its over mantel has disappeared. When in its original position it was a very imposing specimen of Georgian chimney-piece. Made of marble, the two fluted pillars at either side supported an entablature with an oblong medallion in the centre. This held a scene in relief showing a sacrifice to Apollo. When it was removed to the billiard-room, its place was taken by a 'modern' nineteenth century piece.

In the drawing room were the two statuettes by Bertel Thorvaldsen, *Night* and *Morning* which had previously stood in the entrance hall of Tavistock House. There was also, under glass shades, a pair of china figures on gilt stands. With musical evenings being a feature of life at Gad's Hill ("harmony, most evenings" Dickens informed W.H. Russell), the rosewood grand piano was a necessity. To light the evening scenes there were a pair of bronze candelabra with three lights in each, and a gilt girandole (a branched candle-holder) with three brackets for candles. A photograph exists of this room as it was in Dickens' time.

A similar photograph shows Dickens' dining-room with its Spanish mahogany sideboard and the Spanish mahogany dining table. The latter was 14 ft. × 4 ft. 10 in., and there were 10 Spanish mahogany chairs upholstered in crimson morocco leather to go with it. There was a mahogany revolving stand, and a Spanish mahogany three-tier dumb waiter, also a Spanish mahogany screen in three leaves with crimson morocco panels which matched the chair upholstery. Underfoot was a Turkey carpet, 12 ft. 3 in. × 14 ft. 6 in.

The dining room was hung with pictures, many of which can be identified in the photograph. Several visitors remarked on the portrait of *Oliver Cromwell in Armour* by Dobson. There were Frith's paintings of Dolly Varden and Kate Nickleby, Augustus Egg's painting of Dickens in the part of Coldstream in *Used Up*, some pictures by Stanfield – *The Eddystone Lighthouse* and *A Man o' War, A Girl at a Waterfall* by Maclise, depicting the youthful Georgina. Conspicuous in the photograph are Maclise's portrait of Dickens (the 'Nickleby' portrait) and Millais' portrait of Mamie.

Dickens possessed quite a picture gallery, although it is not possible to decide where every item was located. One visitor commented on the "number of Hogarth prints all over the house". He had several drawings by Stanfield – *The Britannia* (in which Dickens and his wife had sailed to America in 1842), *The Land's End*, and *The Logan Rock*, recalling the Cornish holiday with Stanfield, Maclise, and Forster, a drawing of Beauvais Cathedral by Samuel Prout, and two drawings by F.W. Topham, one depicting *Barnaby Rudge and his Mother*, and the other *Little Nell and her Grandfather*. Victorian artists took great delight in the sentimental scenes in Dickens's books. So Dickens had James Hamilton's representation of *What are the Wild Waves Saying?* and Mrs McIan's *Little Nell reading an Inscription on a Tombstone*.

In various rooms were a variety of artistic objects – a two-handled bronze tazza (that is, a shallow saucer-shaped vessel mounted on a foot), a bronze representing an eagle on a rock, and another of a lady, Esmeralda. There was the marble bust of Dickens as a young man by his friend Angus Fletcher, of which Dickens once remarked that it was a good likeness "except for the head". Another marble bust was of Walter Savage Landor, godfather of Dickens' second son. In addition to the Turk with the hookah, there were plaster casts entitled *Cupid and Psyche* and *The Dying Gladiator*.

On the first landing was an illumination, each line of which was executed in a different style of lettering, some of it highly ornate and backed by very intricate designs. It read:

This House
GAD'S HILL PLACE
Stands on the summit of Shakspeare's
Gad's Hill, ever memorable for its
Associations with
Sir John Falstaff, in his noble fancy.

But my lads, my lads, tomorrow morning by four o'clock, early at Gad's Hill! There are pilgirms (sic) going to Canterbury with rich offerings, and traders riding to London with fat purses; I have vizards for you all; you have horses for yourselves.

This was prepared for Dickens by a well-known Victorian artist and designer, Owen Jones, who was responsible for much of the interior decoration of the Crystal Palace. Unfortunately he made a mistake when he had almost completed the lettering and wrote 'pilgirms' instead of 'pilgrims'.

Behind the library was the billiard room which Dickens had originally used as his study. This might account for the splendid fireplace being moved here. Its marble figures in relief were surely in danger once the room was given over to billiards. Installed here was a 7 ft. 6 in. × 4 ft. billiard table (purchased in 1866), and also a Kamptulican round billiard table. The room was equipped with a range of cases and rests, and balls for both billiards and pool. Above the table was a 4-light billiard-room gas burner with four shades. A small flag was kept in this room, and one of the servants was detailed to hoist it on the mast at the top of the house as soon as Dickens arrived, and lower it on his departure.

George Dolby who managed Dickens' reading tours and was invited once or twice to Gad's Hill recorded in his book *Charles Dickens as I Knew Him*: "A peculiarity of the household was the fact that, except at table, no servant was ever seen about. This was because the requirements of life were always ready to hand, especially in the bedrooms. Each of these rooms contained the most comfortable of beds, a sofa and easy-chair, caned-bottom chairs – in which Mr. Dickens had a great belief, always preferring to use one himself – a large-sized writing-table, profusely supplied with paper and envelopes of every conceivable size and description, and an almost daily change of new quill pens. There was a miniature library of books in each room, a comfortable fire in winter, with a shining copper kettle in each fireplace; and on a side-table, cups, saucers, tea-caddy, teapot, sugar and milk, so that this refreshing beverage was always attainable, without even the trouble of asking for it."

With regard to the "miniature library of books" referred to by Dolby, it would seem that Dickens selected the titles to suit, so far as he could judge, the tastes of each guest. Thus Hans Andersen noted that Dickens had placed by his bedside a volume of *The Arabian Nights' Entertainments*, Addison and Steele's *Roger de Coverley* essays, and stories by Washington Irving.

In the basement of the house were the kitchens, pantry, larder, china closet, and the wine cellars. Dickens kept a very good cellar, and drew on it to replenish his wine-cupboard at the *All the Year Round* office. On his death it was well-stocked. The contents were listed in dozens rather than in bottles, e.g. 15 dozen sherry, 4 dozen Old Madeira, 6 dozen Port (22 years in bottle), 16 dozen Medoc, 16 dozen Bourjois, 30 dozen champagne, 14 dozen milk punch, 5 dozen pineapple rum, 27 dozen brandy, 17 dozen whisky, and various other wines and spirits, including some measured not in dozen bottles but in magnums, that is, in 2-quart containers. Thus he had 18 magnums of port and 12 magnums of claret. He had a good quantity of beer on hand also, and it will have been noted that when the nine men had struggled to get the girders in place in the drawing-room, he 'judiciously' refreshed them with three gallons of beer. One can well believe it imparted a festive air – a sort of nine men's morris! He was also generous with the well diggers who having struck water were rewarded with a bottle of gin.

The garden was well-kept, the lawns closely mown, and the flower-beds well stocked with chrysanthemums, azaleas, primulas, geraniums, and burning-bush plants. There was a quantity of garden furniture including a moulded iron table with a revolving top, four portable iron chairs in one of which Dickens was seated when photographed reading to his daughters. There was also a rather large number of mouse-traps – eleven double mouse-traps, twelve spring mouse-traps – together with a rat-trap.

The rats and mice were not the only creatures which stole the master's goods. On one occasion, word reached Dickens' ears that there had been much merry making in a humble cottage in the village when expensive champagne corks were 'flying'. He suspected that he was the provider of this entertainment, and when an inventory of his cellar was taken, he was surprised to learn how little champagne was left. He at once had an extra padlock fitted to the cellar door, but the pilfering continued. Finally, he instructed Georgina to procure a little iron cash box where the cellar-key could be kept. "To that cash-box have two keys, both electrotyped gold. Of those keys you shall always wear one, and I will always wear the other, and the box itself shall be kept, not in your room but in mine, in some drawer that we will settle upon."

Behind the servants' hall was the van-house where a four-wheel spring van was kept. Next to this was the Vinery, divided by a partition into two, in which was a great variety of hot-house plants. Across the yard, where the raven occupied an empty dog-kennel, and the big dogs lay chained but ready to bark fiercely at any intruder, was the coach house.

Dickens had several vehicles in which he could convey his guests. There was a bright red Irish jaunting car with cushions in drab cloth. He had bought this in Belfast and often used it for meeting friends at Higham Station. There was a double-seated basket phaeton, in which he was photographed taking his daughters and sister-in-law for an outing. This had been made in Rochester and was lined in green cloth with cushions to match. His third carriage was a brougham with iron shafts, lined with brown silk. This was a gift from his assistant editor, W.H. Wills. It arrived at Gad's Hill on 29th November 1864. The next day Dickens wrote to Wills:

"I found the beautiful and perfect brougham awaiting me in triumph at the station when I came down yesterday afternoon; Georgina and Marsh both highly mortified that it had fallen dark and the beauties of the carriage were obscured. But of course I had it out in the yard the first thing this morning, and got in and out at both doors, and let down and pulled up the windows, and checked an imaginary coachman, and leaned back in a state of placid contemplation. It is the lightest and prettiest and best carriage of the class, ever made. . . ."

During his thirteen years of occupancy, Dickens must have had a succession of horses. We know he had to sell one pony which kicked its stall to pieces, and that he occasionally hired a horse from Rochester when one of his own was out of condition. Among the occupants of his stables were a reliable grey cob called Trotty Veck, a carriage horse named Toby, Mamie's saddle horse, Boy, and a lively pony named Newman Noggs. Towards the end of Dickens' life, Newman Noggs became old and infirm, and reluctantly his owner had to have him put down. Many visitors remarked on the musical jingle which announced the arrival of Dickens' carriage at the station. Amongst the various harnesses, saddles, reins, etc. in the stables was a set of carriage bells.

Dickens turned out his stable-man very smartly, as may be seen from the photograph of the man who is holding the horse while Dickens prepares to go driving in his basket phaeton. Dickens related an amusing story about this man, although the event cannot have been very amusing for Georgina who was not at all well when it occurred (October, 1862): "Georgina being left alone here the other day, was done no good to by a great consternation among the servants. On going downstairs, she found Marsh (the stableman) seated with great dignity and anguish in an armchair, and incessantly crying out: 'I am dead.' To which the women servants said, with great pathos (and with some appearance of reason): 'No, you ain't, Marsh!' And to which he persisted in replying: 'Yes, I am; I am dead!' Some neighbouring vagabond was impressed to drive a cart over to Rochester and fetch the doctor, who said (the patient and his consolers being all very anxious that the heart should be the scene of affliction): 'Stomach!' "

Beyond the wall and behind the coach-house was the croquet lawn, and at the opposite side of the house was a much larger area where there were fruit trees and a kitchen garden. Behind the house extended some 26 acres of the meadow and arable land. Dickens was careful to get two crops of hay each year, and restricted the use of his land for cricket matches in order to achieve this. He did, however, sponsor the local team by permitting them to play here.

The tunnel mentioned at the beginning of this chapter was constructed after permission had been obtained from the local authority. Dickens' brother, Alfred, in co-operation with Henry Austin, designed and supervised the work. The tunnel was lined with bricks; steps led down from the lawn and up into the shrubbery (or wilderness) beyond. The habits of the men engaged in the work of construction (and it has to be remembered that this was a period of great activity in railway and tunnel construction) greatly interested and amused Dickens. In the *Uncommercial Traveller* paper on 'Tramps', he noted:

"Bricklayers often tramp, in twos and threes, lying by night in their 'lodges', which are scattered all over the country. Bricklaying is another of the occupations that can by no means be transacted in rural parts, without the assistance of spectators – of as many as can be convened. In thinly-peopled spots, I have known bricklayers on tramp, coming up with bricklayers at work, to be so sensible of the indispensability of lookers-on, that they themselves have sat up in that capacity, and have been unable to subside into the acceptance of a proffered share in the job, for two or three days together. Sometimes the 'navvy', on tramp, with an extra pair of half-boots over his shoulder, a bag, a bottle, and a can, will take a similar part in a job of excavation, and will look at it without engaging in it, until all his money is gone."

That this was the case with the excavation and bricklaying necessary in the construction of the tunnel was admitted in the next sentence:

"The current of my uncommercial pursuits caused me only last summer to want a little body of workmen for a certain spell of work, in a pleasant part of the country; and I was at one time honoured with the attendance of as many as seven-and-twenty, who were looking at six."

Within the shrubbery, which was surrounded by iron railings, was a profusion of shrubs and bushes, all of them dominated by two huge cedars. The branches of these had proliferated, and the lateral shoots from near the base of the trunks had thickened and spread. Until Dickens took over the land, this was indeed a wilderness, but with access through the tunnel it proved the ideal site on which he might erect the chalet presented to him in 1865 by his friend, Charles Fechter, the actor. This arrived one day in fifty or more packing cases, delivered to Higham station and needing transportation up to the house. There were 94 pieces to be assembled, but first a brick foundation was needed. The project turned out to be far more costly than Dickens had expected. Altogether, what with the tunnel and the erection of the chalet, he must have spent a considerable amount of money on the Wilderness.

However, the chalet proved a great asset. Dickens fitted up the top room with a small table on which was placed a writing-slope. (He preferred to write on a sloping surface.) He brought in a couch and chairs, and placed large mirrors around the walls to reflect the trees. Here he did much of his work on the days he was at Gad's Hill during the last few years of his life.

CHAPTER 4

Life at Gad's Hill Place

Dickens used Gad's Hill as a place to relax, a place where he could be the country squire, interesting himself in country matters – hay-making, tramps, trees and gardens. He could invite people down for the weekend, sometimes for longer, and take them on walks about the neighbourhood or, if they were specially-favoured visitors, arrange jaunts for them through Rochester to Canterbury.

Gad's Hill saw only one aspect of Dickens. He spent much of his time in London, working in the office of *All the Year Round*, sleeping in the flat above the office, and directing affairs at Gad's Hill by correspondence with Georgina. While in London he was a frequent attender at the theatre, often dined out with friends, and was an honoured guest at more formal functions. Dickens was much in demand too as a public speaker. He also spent a considerable time out of London, especially in later years, on reading tours in England and America.

There were the two public aspects of Dickens – the country squire at Gad's Hill, and the editor and public reader in London and elsewhere. But there was a strictly private aspect about which we know very little – the Dickens who secretly visited Ellen Ternan at Slough and later at Peckham, the Dickens who maintained a little country cottage at Condette outside Boulogne and who would mysteriously 'disappear' from time to time.

His absences being so frequent, casual callers were indeed fortunate if they found the master of Gad's Hill at home. Mr. W. E. Church and his two companions were such callers. They had set out on a walking tour of Kent, and found themselves (as they had probably intended) at the Sir John Falstaff tavern enjoying glasses of ale and surveying the novelist's domain across the road. They decided to send a note across and solicit an introduction. Accordingly they penned and signed the following: "Three admirers of the genius of Charles Dickens desire to pay their devoted regards to him." A young woman from the tavern delivered it, and shortly came back with the message that Dickens would see them as soon as he had finished writing a letter. They were so delighted with their success that they shook hands with each other, laughing and grimacing with excitement.

Dickens met them on the gravel drive in front of the house. He was wearing a grey tweed suit and a round bowler hat, the garb in which he was photographed several times at Gad's Hill. He greeted them kindly, saying, "I am glad to see you. Come to taste our Kentish air, have you?" As he showed them around the grounds they discussed the locations of several scenes in his novels, and he amazed them with his detailed knowledge of London topography. He conducted them down the steps and through the tunnel to enable them to see the chalet and the Wilderness. The callers were rather overwhelmed in the presence of so famous a man and were anxious not to prolong their visit in case they took up too much of his valuable time. But when they murmured that perhaps they would be intruding if they remained longer, Dickens rejoined with a laugh: "No, no! Not at all! I have greatly enjoyed seeing you." At the gate, he shook hands warmly with each one of them in turn. The young men were quite overcome by his kindness, and at a loss how to thank him. They could only bow and go on their way.

Guests who stayed at the house had more information to impart. Most of them mentioned how they reached it, some of them who were visitors to England being actually met at a London railway station. The Nortons, for example, from the United States were met in London and given a warm welcome to England. Mrs. Norton recorded that he looked "fresh and brisk in a suit of grey linen and felt hat to match, a flower in his buttonhole, his hands on his hips, his eyes intently fixed on the crowd." Being a regular user of the railway he was able to command a private compartment should he desire one. (When he learned of Jerrold's death, he was obviously sharing the compartment with others.) While escorting the Nortons to Higham he pointed out the engineering of the roads to the east of London. He spoke of his recent visit to the United States, and his desire to make a similar tour of Australia where his son, Alfred, had already settled and where his youngest son was soon to follow. He spoke very candidly about George Henry Lewes and George Eliot, whom he referred to as the Leweses. Acknowledging that they were a very talented couple (and he had been the first to suspect that George Eliot was in fact a woman) he went on to say: "They really are the ugliest couple in London." When the train reached Higham they found the basket phaeton awaiting them. Dickens "jumped on to the box and we rattled off to Gad's Hill." Other guests were met at Higham by Dickens driving his Irish jaunting car. George Dolby recorded being met on several occasions and being taken on a "drive through the pleasantest of the Kentish country, either on an 'outside' Irish jaunting car, or, in fine weather, in a basket carriage, with the nattiest of ponies . . . or in wet weather, with a brougham drawn by the most knowing and best-trained of cobs with a 'hogmain'; always escorted by three or four enormous dogs of the Mount St. Bernard, mastiff, or Newfoundland species."

From Mrs. Susan Norton we learn that "upstairs over the library was Mamie's bedroom, pretty and French like herself; over the drawing-room Georgina's, and over the dining-room Mr. Dickens'." Dickens' room was therefore the large one at the rear of the house with windows commanding wonderful views towards Rochester and across the countryside to the south. From Mrs. Norton comes the further information that at the time of their visit, Dickens used his bedroom as a study. Other informants also recorded that he often worked in his bedroom, so perhaps neither the library nor the upper room of the chalet were his principal work-places. Mrs. Norton noted:

"The furniture was simple, the walls were covered with engravings from Hogarth; his dressing-room, which was only partitioned from the room, he had covered on the inside with wood-cuts from Leech which he had pasted on himself. On his bed lay a brilliant bit of oriental covering. . . . In the large window looking towards Rochester stood his perfectly simple unornamented leather-covered writing table."

Francis Finlay, editor of the Belfast newspaper *The Northern Whig*, visited Gad's Hill in June 1862, some years before the Nortons, and sent a friend a memorandum of his stay:

Monday – Left London Bridge station at 2.30 and at Higham station was met by Charles Dickens in his Irish car. Drove me over to Gad's Hill Place where was most kindly received by Mary Dickens, Georgina Hogarth, and Mrs. Charles Collins (formerly Kate Dickens). Introduced to Charles Collins. Played several games of billiard bagatelle with Charles Dickens and afterwards with Charles Collins. Dinner at 6. Took in Mary Dickens. Everything very nice. Very pleasant talk. Played whist in the evening, and had a lot of chat before going to bed at 11.30. *Tuesday* – After breakfast walked about the grounds, chatted, wrote letters, and in the afternoon drove in to Gravesend with Dickens to meet Mrs. Thos. A. Trollope. . . . Came home with him to lunch, and then we all went to play croquet on the lawn, in which we were busily engaged, with great spirit, when Mr. Fechter arrived. The game went on till dinner when Captain Goff came up from Chatham and Frank Dickens from London. Dinner exceedingly elegant, and a profusion of good talk, Fechter being admirable. After dinner croquet again until it was too dark to see any more, and then we all came in and played a most lively game of vingt-et-un until bedtime. *Wednesday* – After breakfast we had croquet as usual, performed by the whole party . . . we had lunch at 1.0 . . . [in the afternoon] Charles Dickens, Charles Collins, Miss Hogarth and I went out for a stroll, got caught in a tremendous shower, and were drenched. Came home, changed and dined (elegantly as usual) and after dinner we had some 'bounding ball' practice on the lawn, by Charles Dickens, Frank Dickens and Charles Collins and myself, very good exercise indeed. Chat in the evening and whist, Dickens and I partners against Miss Hogarth and Charles Collins. In the evening had a very long and agreeable talk with Miss Hogarth, . . . who is a really delightful person, plain, unassuming, totally unaffected and of singularly pleasant and easy manner. After whist, a long chat, telling stories, riddles and conundrums and to bed at 11. . . . *Thursday* – The whole pleasant party broke up. Mr. and Mrs. Collins went home to Hyde Park Gate. Miss Hogarth and Dickens to Wellington Street, and I back to Sloane Street.

[Fechter, Thomas Trollope and Mamie had left on Wednesday.]

Dickens was very fond of riddles and conundrums, and many visitors recalled taking part in guessing and memory games at Gad's Hill. Dickens himself was adept at a game which Percy Fitzgerald described:

"After dinner we had small plays, one in which he exhibited singular cleverness, viz. that of guessing a subject fixed on when he was out of the

The library showing Dickens' desk and the door with the dummy bookbacks. From the painting by Luke Fildes, *The Empty Chair*.

The dining-room at Gad's Hill Place.

The drawing-room as extended by Dickens.

The chalet. (This photo shows it in Cobham Woods, but it must have appeared like this while in the shrubbery at Gad's Hill.)

View of Dickens' writing table etc. in the top room of his chalet.

room, in half a dozen questions. I have often seen this performed, but never in so masterly a style, for it is a test of character, and proves a power of getting at the essence of things. His selection of subjects to puzzle others when their turn came was characteristically ingenious – 'The Lantern in a Railway Guard's Hand'; 'The Gunpowder used in the Gunpowder Plot' (we got as far as 'Guy Fawkes' but no farther). He told how he piqued himself on a former occasion on a great triumph – the discovery of a regular poser: 'The Boot on the off-leg of a Postillion.'"

Another parlour game was recalled by Harry Dickens:

"One of the party started by giving a name, such as, for instance, Napoleon. The next person had to repeat this and add something of his own, such as Napoleon, Blackbeetle, and so on, until the string of words began to get long and difficult to remember. My father, after many turns, had successfully gone through the long string of words, and finished up with his own contribution, 'Warren's Blacking, 30, Strand.' He gave this with an odd twinkle in his eye and a strange inflection in his voice which at once forcibly arrested my attention and left a vivid impression on my mind for some time afterwards. Why, I could not, for the life of me, understand." None of the family knew, at this time, of Dickens' boyhood experiences in the blacking warehouse.

Although there are frequent references to his playing whist and other card games, some of his family believed he did not really like playing cards. According to Mamie, he also disliked croquet, although he seems to have joined in the contests often enough. He enjoyed watching cricket, and encouraged the local team by permitting them to play on his field. His younger boys seem to have spent much of their summer holidays at cricket, and if not shouting in the field were clumping up and down stairs to their father's annoyance. He therefore felt the need to bring some discipline into the home. "As we small boys were somewhat slack and untidy," his son Harry recalled, "a system was set on foot which went by the name of 'Pegs, Parade, and Custos'. To each boy was allotted a particular peg for his hat and coat; there was a parade from time to time in order to check the stains of grease or dirt which had accumulated on our clothing; and to one boy was allotted the task each week of collecting the sticks, balls, and croquet and cricket materials which represented the 'Custos' for the week."

Percy Fitzgerald, who was often at Gad's Hill in the later years and whom Dickens would probably have liked to see as a son-in-law, recalled:

"a cricket match – 'the Higham Eleven' against some other competitors – which drew an attendance of villagers and others. Dickens treated it with a grave solemnity that was amusing, and enjoyed the proceedings heartily. There was the umpire's marquee pitched, chairs arranged, flags flying. We even got up a sort of eager enthusiasm. Our host himself officiated as marker (scorer). I see him in his white jean coat, and his grey hat set a little on one side, his double glasses on, going conscientiously through his work; scoring down 'byes' and 'overs' and runs; at times cheering some indifferent hit with an encouraging 'Well run! well run!' This he kept up the whole day. He was partial to marking. There were plenty of cooling drinks on the ground, a cask of beer for the crowd, and some wonderful cup, for which he had some special receipt – as he had for everything else."

Dickens did indeed have a special 'receipt', recipe, or secret, for many things. This recipe referred to by Fitzgerald was possibly for the drink which came to be known in the family as Aunt Georgie's Cider Cup, composed of sherry and brandy in addition to cider. Dickens also taught the servants a special way of folding the dinner serviettes, and as one of his maids remembered, "Lord Darnley's servants were always anxious to learn how the folding was done, but they never discovered the secret." This maid also recalled that "at dinner-parties it was the custom to place a little buttonhole for each guest. This was mostly made up of scarlet geranium (Dickens' favourite flower), with a bit of the leaf and a frond of maidenhair fern."

Dickens' eldest daughter, who was the official hostess at Gad's Hill even though Georgina was mainly responsible for the management, published an article in the Philadelphia *Ladies Home Journal* some years after her father's death. In it she wrote:

"In very many of my father's books there are frequent references to delicious meals, wonderful dinners, and more marvellous dishes, steaming bowls of punch, etc. which have led many to believe that he was a man very fond of the table. And yet I think no more abstemious man ever lived. In the Gad's Hill days when the house was full of visitors, he had a peculiar notion of always having the menu for the day's dinner placed on the sideboard at luncheon time. And then he would discuss every item in his fanciful humorous way with his guests, much to this effect: 'Cock-a-leekie? Good, decidedly good! Fried soles with shrimp sauce? Good again! Croquettes of chicken; Weak, very weak! Decided want of imagination here!' and so on. And he would apparently be so taken up with the merits or demerits of a menu that one might imagine he lived for nothing but the coming dinner. He had a small but healthy appetite, but was remarkably abstemious both in eating and drinking."

Copies of his menu cards have been preserved. They were headed with his crest – the lion couchant, holding in its dexter paw a Maltese cross – the device which also appeared on his crockery, and was engraved on his cutlery. (And was also printed on his book-plates.) His entitlement to such a crest has been disputed, but Dickens' response to enquirers on the subject was that his father had always used it, and therefore . . .

Dickens was the perfect host. This is borne out by every account we have of him. The best is perhaps that of Susan Norton (wife of Charles Eliot Norton), who described a dinner party at Gad's Hill:

"At seven o'clock we all reassembled, a large party, with other guests, among them officers from Chatham, one of them with his young wife, a stranger to everybody. Dickens, punctual to the minute, came in fresh, animated, alive to everyone's interest, and in a moment had roused us completely – no-one was to go to sleep there."

This took place, it should be noted, when Dickens had hardly recovered from the exhausting experience of his American series of readings, when his leg was giving him trouble, and when he was really, beneath the facade, a chronically ill man. Mrs. Norton continued:

"The little lady from Chatham and I sat on either side of him at dinner – his vivacity never flagged, nor was it for one person alone. He appeared to hear what everyone at the table said, and turned from one end of it to the other with the utmost rapidity, told stories, talked tête à tête, gave a toast, in short was the life of the dinner and without seeming to make any effort or even talking in loud boisterous tones. Of course, every one was likely to be silent when he talked, but then he never when liveliest was noisy. After dinner the gentlemen soon came into the drawing-room, and again Dickens seemed entirely given up to the interests of his guests, attentive to the officer's wife (a dull little woman with a decoration of lockets which amused him) and indeed to everyone, the stupidest not excepted. We all stood for a time round the piano playing at words with letters. Very soon Dickens moved off to talk to the little lady who was too shy to play, but whom he evidently managed to set at her ease, and then, seeing that my forces had given out, he came and sat down by me taking Georgina's place and sending her off to his first charge."

This was rather a special occasion when two important American visitors were staying with him. On less formal occasions, especially when the guests were predominantly male, the evenings would pass much as Dolby described them:

". . . the gentlemen adjourned to the billiard-room, where, before going to bed, some little time was spent in the enjoyment of some excellent cigars and a walk round the table to the click of the balls, either in a game at pool or a contest at billiards, Mr. Dickens being fond of contests, for he used to say, 'it brings out the mettle!'" (He does not appear to have been a particularly good player, however. Marcus Stone seems to have been the champion.) "Then, so far as the host was concerned, the day was done, for it was his invariable habit to retire to bed at midnight – but without imposing any condition upon his guests that they should follow his example – the most intimate of his male friends present, if none of his sons were there, being delegated 'host' in his absence, with strict injunctions to 'see the gas out all right' and to take great care of the keys of the sideboard until morning."

Mamie Dickens re-affirming that her father was delightful as a host, went on:

"But when he was most delightful, was alone with us at home and sitting over dessert, and when my sister was with us especially . . . for she had great power in 'drawing him out'. At such times although he might sit down to dinner in a grave or abstracted mood, he would invariably soon throw aside his silence and end by delighting us all with his genial talk and his quaint fancies about people and things."

Dickens spent most of his Christmases and New Year's Days at home while he was at Gad's Hill. Mamie recollected:

"Our house was always filled with guests, while a cottage in the village was reserved for the use of the bachelor members of our holiday party. My father himself always deserted work for the week and that was almost our greatest treat. He was the fun and life of those gatherings, the true Christmas spirit of sweetness and hospitality filling his large and generous heart."

A letter to Georgina from Dickens who was then at the Adelphi Hotel in Liverpool reveals how Dickens prepared well in advance for the festivities. The letter, dated 29th October 1868, reads: "Writing to Ellis (his wine-merchant) for one cask of wine, and remembering Christmas, I altered my intention and ordered two. Perhaps their arrival may already have astonished you."

Mamie's account continues:

"Long walks with him were daily treats to be remembered. Games passed our evenings merrily. 'Proverbs', a game of memory, was very popular, and it was one in which either my aunt or myself was apt to prove winner. Father's annoyance at our failure sometimes was very amusing, but quite genuine. 'Dumb Crambo' was another favourite, and one in which my father's great imitative ability showed finely. I remember one evening his dumb showing of the word 'frog' was so extremely laughable that the memory of it convulsed Marcus Stone. . . .

On Christmas Day we all had our glasses filled, and then my father, raising his, would say: 'Here's to us all. God bless us!' a toast which was rapidly and willingly drunk. His conversation, as may be imagined, was often extremely humorous, and I have seen the servants, who were waiting at table, convulsed with laughter at his droll remarks and stories."

Dickens was in Scotland just before Christmas Day 1868, but completed the readings there in time to return home for the festivities. His manager, George Dolby, was invited to join the party at Gad's Hill, but being unable to do so, promised to provide the turkey. Accordingly, on reaching his home at Ross-on-Wye, he ordered a 30lb bird and sent it off by rail. A day or two later he was shocked to receive the following letter from Dickens:

WHERE
IS
THAT
TURKEY
IT
HAS
NOT
ARRIVED
!!!!!!!!!!!!

Alas, the railway-van in which it was travelling had caught fire and been detained at Reading, the charred remains of the turkey being sold off at about six-pence to the poor people of that town.

New Year's Eve was another special occasion. The family and guests would assemble in the drawing-room, playing cards or the games already described, until just before midnight when the manservant would sound the gong in the hall and throw open the door so that everyone could come out and join the servants there. Dickens would get out his watch and everyone would wait expectantly for the hall clock to strike and the village bells to ring out. Then, exclaiming 'A happy New Year to us all. God bless us!' he would begin shaking hands all round, kissing the ladies and leading off the dance – sometimes starting off with the cook as his partner. At Gad's Hill Dickens played at being Mr. Wardle at Manor Farm.

Like Mr. Wardle, Dickens enjoyed taking a long walk through the countryside, and often his guests would accompany him. He would vary the direction of his walks, some days going down towards the marshes where Pip had met the convict, on others going through Rochester, calling perhaps at the Crispin and Crispianus Inn in Strood on his way back. The landlord there remembered Dickens, and later gave a rather unflattering description of him as

"usually wearing low shoes not over-well mended, loose large check-patterned trousers that sometimes got entangled in the shoes when walking, a house coat thrown open, sometimes without waistcoat, a belt instead of braces, a necktie which now and then got round towards his ear, and a large-brimmed felt hat, similar to an American's, set well at the back of his head. In his hand he carried by the middle an umbrella, which he was in the habit of constantly swinging, and if he had dogs (a not unfrequent occurrence), he had a small whip as well. He walked in the middle of the road at a rapid pace, upright, but with his eyes cast down as if in deep thought. When he called at the Crispin for refreshments, usually a glass of ale (mild sixpenny – bitter ale was not drawn in those days), or a little cold brandy and water, he walked straight in, and sat down at the corner of the settle on the right-hand side where the arm is, opposite the fireplace; he rarely spoke to anyone, but looked round as though taking in everything at a glance."

One of Dickens' favourite walks was to Cobham, a place he had made famous in *The Pickwick Papers*. Mr. Tupman fled there to hide from the world at the Leather Bottle Inn after he had been disappointed in his love-affair with the spinster aunt. Dickens mentioned it again in his Christmas story, 'The Seven Poor Travellers': "As for me, I was going to walk, by Cobham Woods, as far upon my way to London as I fancied. ... By Cobham Hall I came to the village, and the churchyard where the dead had been quietly buried . . ." Dickens' eldest son confirmed that "Down the lanes, and through the park to Cobham, was always a favourite walk with Charles Dickens; and he never wearied of acting as cicerone to his guests to its fine church and the quaint almshouses with the disused refectory behind." Knowing his love of the park, his neighbour, the Earl of Darnley, gave him a key so that he could gain admission whenever he wished.

Many of Dickens' friends have left records of their walks with him, but not all could keep up his pace, nor go the distances he liked to cover. A guest who really amazed him was the music critic, Henry Fothergill Chorley, who was tall and thin and apparently frail, but managed to keep up a good pace over a walk of 22 miles, afterwards appearing not the least the worse for it.

Dickens' dogs often accompanied him. He had several while he was at Gad's Hill, they being necessary for the protection of the property and its inmates. His daughter, Mamie, also had a dog – a white Pomeranian called Mrs. Bouncer – which can be seen on some of the group photographs taken in the garden.

The first dogs he had here were a bloodhound named Turk and a St. Bernard named Linda. On one of their walks through the Cobham lanes both these dogs cut their feet and had to limp home. Turk featured in Dickens' correspondence on another occasion when, to the horror of the family, he produced some eighteen feet of worms from his mouth. In July 1865 Turk was killed by a railway train and Linda just managed to escape.

The next dogs to be acquired were Newfoundlands – Don and his son, a puppy named Bumble. These were the two which came to meet Dickens at Gravesend when he returned from America and trotted alongside the basket phaeton, lifting their heads up now and again to have their ears pulled. During the drought in the summer of 1868, Dickens would not let the dogs swim in the canal because the village people had to drink from it. He wrote to James T. Fields in Boston:

"But when the dogs get into the Medway it is hard to get them out again. The other day Bumble (the son, Newfoundland dog) got into difficulties among some floating timber, and became frightened. Don (the father) was standing by me, shaking off the wet and looking on carelessly, when all of a sudden he perceived something amiss, and went in with a bound and brought Bumble out by the ear. The scientific way in which he towed him along was charming."

Then Percy Fitzgerald decided to make Dickens a gift of an Irish bloodhound named Sultan. It was a splendid animal which Dickens greatly admired, but was most ferocious. No sooner had he arrived in September 1865 than he attempted to swallow Mrs. Bouncer. By December, Dickens could report to Fitzgerald:

"Sultan has grown immensely, and is a sight. But he is so accursedly fierce towards other dogs, that I am obliged to take him out muzzled. Also he has an invincible repugnance to soldiers, which, in a military country, is inconvenient. Such is the spirit of the dog that, with his muzzle tight on, he dashed into the heart of a company in heavy marching order (only the other day) and pulled down an objectionable private. Except under such provocations, he is as gentle and docile with me, as a dog can possibly be. Last night, the gardener fired at some man in the garden, upon whom he came suddenly, and who attacked him in a desperate manner. I immediately turned out, unloosed Sultan and hunted the vagabond. We couldn't get hold of him, but the intelligence of the dog, and the delighted confidence he imparted to me, as he tumbled across the country in the dark, were quite enchanting. Two policemen appearing in the distance and making a professional show of stealthiness, had a narrow escape. As he was in the act of flying at them, I was obliged to hold him round the neck with both arms . . . and call to the Force to vanish in an inglorious manner."

Sultan, unfortunately, was too dangerous to survive. He was suspected of having bolted a blue-eyed kitten, and (as Dickens said) "making me acquainted with the circumstance by his agonies of remorse (or indigestion?)". He also broke loose on several occasions, and though muzzled came back covered with blood. Fitzgerald related the rest:

"He went off one day to have a sort of prize-fight with a dog of his own size, weight, and age, residing some distance off, of whom he was jealous, and after a terrible battle left him almost dead. Yet his master still clung to him. Indeed, no dog ever had such a chance, or was more tolerated. But at last it came to a fatal point beyond which toleration could not safely go. One day a scream was heard at the gate, and those who rushed out found that the dog had seized a neighbour's child by the leg."

Dickens hauled the dog away and beat it, but it was clear that punishment would have no lasting effect. The next day the decision was taken to order Sultan's execution. He was led away in the morning by the gardener to the end of the meadow and shot. One of the family wrote later: "The gardener took him as far away from the house as he could to kill him, still we all heard the shot, and I can't tell you how terrible it was."

Horses and dogs were not the only animals at Gad's Hill. There was a raven, the last of a line, but a quieter one than its predecessors, with none of their cork-drawing imitations or declarations that "I'm a devil". This one appears to have lived a retired life in an old dog-kennel and to have survived to an older age than the others. There was also a canary named Dick – "our wonderful little Dick", his owner called him when he was recounting the attacks on the bird by two tigerish and fearful cats and French's attempts to shoot them. When Dick passed away at the age of 15, he was buried under a rose-tree in a quiet corner of the garden and a little wooden head-board erected to mark the grave. The epitaph read:

This is
the grave of
DICK
the best of birds
born
at Broadstairs
Midsummer 1851
died
at Gad's Hill Place,
4th October 1866.

There were also two pet cats. Dickens was not at first very partial to cats because they were a danger to his canary. But when Georgina was given a little white kitten he relented, and soon became as fond of Williamina (as the kitten was named) as the kitten became fond of him. When Williamina produced kittens, she was granted the tremendous privilege of living in his study – and maybe it was one of her litter, the blue-eyed kitten, which was devoured by the savage Sultan. All of her kittens, save one, were given away. The one which remained was completely deaf, but it became extremely devoted to Dickens, followed him about and sat with him. When he was writing of an evening by candlelight, it had a habit of jumping on the table, and with a quick dab of a paw, extinguishing the flame. It was never given a name, but was known as The Master's Cat.

Mention has already been made of some of the servants. French figures a number of times in anecdotes about the early years at Gad's Hill, but he did not stay. He injured himself and was not able (according to Dickens) to "carry heavy family trays about". So when Sir Edward Bulwer Lytton was looking for a trusty and versatile servant, Dickens recommended him warmly, and French obtained the post. Dickens wrote to Lytton:

"He was in France with me, as well as in England. He was a remarkably willing, active and ready fellow; and everybody who used to come here liked him and noticed him. . . . He is well used to a literary man's ways, has capital notions of keeping people out who want to get in, and got a knowledge of a number of public faces here which was very useful. . . . Also, in Paris, he kept his account in French money in a very knowing way, and could make himself understood anywhere." So when, two and half years later, French threw up his job with Lytton, Dickens was amazed. "I too thought he was yours for life. . . . I am afraid I do not know of a successor whom I could of my own knowledge and experience recommend. An English man-servant who can make his way abroad and make the best of it, is so very rare an article. And I have been so fortunate in servants, that French and two other men (one dead, and the other with me now after eighteen years), are all I can be said to have had."

It will be seen that French had held a rather special position, part valet, part courier (like the deceased Roche, the 'brave Courier' of *Pictures from Italy*). His position was taken by a man who must at first have been in Dickens' employment concurrently with French. This was John Thompson who remained with Dickens for 25 years. Although his work was largely away from Gad's Hill, at the office in Wellington Street, and on reading tours, he was well known to the family. He, in fact, was the man who sounded the gong on New Year's Eves. Dickens described him as "the cleverest man of his kind in the world, and can do anything, from excellent carpentry to excellent cookery". Sad to say, Dickens discovered he had been robbing the cash-box and felt he had no option but to dismiss him. He was anxious, however, to keep the details from the servants at Gad's Hill. Writing from London, he instructed Georgina to devise some story such as that "John is going into some small business – anything of that kind," and he told Mamie: "No third person who knew him through his old long service should witness John's shame."

William Hughes, whose book *A Week's Tramp in Dickens Land* is a mine of information, interviewed two Higham ladies who had been parlour-maids at Gad's Hill. The first, Mrs. Easedown, had left to be married on the day Dickens had his fatal seizure. He had given her an autographed photograph of himself as a parting gift. She recalled that on the previous Monday morning he had ordered breakfast to be ready throughout the week at 7.30 am (sharp) instead of the usual 9.00, saying he had so much to do before Friday.

The other lady, Mrs. Wright, had lived four years at Gad's Hill. She remembered

"at the time of her engagement as parlour-maid, that the servants told her to let a gentleman in at the front door who was approaching. She didn't know who it was, as she had never seen Mr. Dickens before. She opened the door, and the gentleman entered in a very upright manner, and after thanking her, looked hard at her, and then walked upstairs. On returning to the kitchen, the servants asked her who it was that had just come in. She replied, 'I don't know, but I think it was the master.' 'Did he speak?' they asked. 'No,' said she, 'but he looked at me in a very determined way.' Said they, 'He was reading your character, and he now knows you thoroughly', or words to that effect. . . . On one occasion in her early days, the dinner-lift (to the use of which she was unaccustomed) broke and ran down quickly, smashing the crockery and bruising her arm. Mr. Dickens jumped up quickly and said, 'Never mind the breakage; is your arm hurt?' As it was painful, he immediately applied arnica to the bruise, and gave her a glass of port wine."

With quite a large garden, orchard and lawns, Dickens needed to employ a gardener and one or two boys to assist him. The last gardener he had was an experienced and enterprising man named George Brunt, who was helped by a thirteen-year old lad, George Woolley. Brunt was a literate man, so when Dickens was staying in London in the spring, he would send Brunt notes about getting the garden ready for the summer. On 13th April 1870, Dickens commended his gardener, saying:

"I think your idea, Brunt, of partitioning the Vinery and so getting our hothouse *a very good one*. I have begged Messrs. Cottam and Co. to send down to make an estimate for the cost of the work, which I have told them you will describe exactly. Remember that I want to avoid unnecessary expense, and that what we want is merely to have efficient means of preparing plants for the conservatory."

Another note to Brunt, dated less that four weeks before Dickens' death, indicates Dickens' close supervision of all things pertaining to the garden, and his constant watch on expenditure.

"I enclose you a cheque, Brunt, for Seven Pounds. I will speak to Miss Mary at dinner time today about the Hanging Baskets for the conservatory. You may get some hardy Ferns from Illmans for the rock work. Be careful not to get more than are absolutely necessary, as the garden expenses are becoming excessively heavy. Miss Hogarth tells me that you want 18 more Mrs. Pollock Geraniums and 12 Lavender Plants. You may get them from Illmans too."

The stableman, Marsh, has already been mentioned. The other male servants were the house-boy, Isaac Armitage, and the undergardener, George Woolley. Details of others are difficult to ascertain, although in Dickens' letters there are mentions of James, Barker, and Bottle, and there was Emma, a maid, and Catherine, the cook. Dickens cared for them all, however, when he made his will, leaving "the sum of 19 guineas to each and every domestic servant, male and female, who shall be in my employment at the time of my decease, and shall have been in my employment for not less than a period of one year." Evidently, all the servants, with the exception of George Woolley, came within this category, and Georgina seems to have made some provision for George. He lived for many years afterwards, and was photographed when an old man of 86 holding a cup and saucer which had once belonged to his old employer.

"He was a toff, he was," he told an interviewer. "Opposite the house was a sort of wood the master called the Wilderness. He used to go over there to write. I used to hear what sounded like someone making a speech. I wondered what it was at first, and then I found out it was Mr. Dickens composing his writing out loud. He was working on *The Mystery of Edwin Drood* then."

It would be wrong to suppose because of the many references to the genial host, the charming daughters, the well-ordered household, etc. etc. that life at Gad's Hill Place was idyllic. No doubt the accounts of visits to the house are fairly accurate, for Dickens did not parade his difficulties and his visitors might not have realised the strains and sadnesses which his ebullient exterior disguised. But in many ways, his life from the time he moved in was darkened.

It was darkened, inevitably, by his separation from Catherine and the disturbances which accompanied it – the departure of Charley to stay with his mother, the knowledge that Katey sided with her mother and visited her contrary to her father's wishes, the difficult position of Georgina who remained as housekeeper, and the estrangement with several old friends.

Catherine saw very little of Gad's Hill Place. She was there in the summer of 1857 for a month or two; that was all.

The guests who now came to Gad's Hill were mostly a new group of friends. Although John Forster did not sever relations, his place as Dickens' holiday companion was taken by Wilkie Collins. Men such as Fechter, Chorley, Fitzgerald, Edmund Yates and Marcus Stone took the place of Ainsworth, Maclise, Browne and Stanfield. Many old friends had passed away; others such as Macready were lingering on in retirement. In 1852 when Dickens heard of Count D'Orsay's death, he had exclaimed: "Poor D'Orsay! It is a tremendous consideration that friends should fall around us in such awful numbers as we attain middle life. What a field of battle it is!" As the years passed he was to be saddened by many more falling around him, including his son Walter, his mother, his three surviving brothers, his brother-in-law Henry Austin, and old friends such as Landor, Douglas Jerrold, Leigh Hunt and Leech to name but a few.

The family had not been at Gad's Hill two months when Walter departed for India. Unfortunately, he did not prosper there. Although he was promoted to Lieutenant in the 42nd Highlanders, he remained very low on the list for a captaincy, and, what was most worrying for his father, he began to get into debt. His elder brother, Charley, while travelling home from China in 1861, met him, stayed with him a week or two, and paid his debts. But Walter was soon in debt again, and promised he would not write home until he was financially in the clear. So no news arrived at Gad's Hill until he wrote to say he had been ill and was being sent home on sick leave. Sadly, before he could embark, he died on 31st December 1863 in the officers' hospital in Calcutta. This news did not reach England until 7th February in the following year. (Things chanced to happen on Dickens' birthday.)

Walter's death came as a grievous blow. Dickens could not help remembering how gaily the rest of the family had spent that New Year's Eve at Gad's Hill while Walter was suffering his fatal seizure.

"On the last night of the old year I was acting charades with all my children," he wrote to Miss Coutts. "I had made something to carry, as the Goddess of Discord; and it came into my head as it stood against the wall while I was dressing, that it was like the dismal things that are carried at Funerals. I took a pair of scissors and cut away a quantity of black calico that was upon it, to remove this likeness. But while I was using it, I noticed that its *shadow* on the wall still had that resemblance, though the thing itself had not. And when I went to bed it was in my bedroom, and still looked so like, that I took it to pieces before I went to sleep. All this would have been exactly the same, if poor Walter had *not* died that night."

To make matters worse, Dickens had only just (in January) bade goodbye to his third son, Frank, who had obtained an appointment in the Bengal Mounted Police. This boy would be arriving in Calcutta eagerly expecting to see his brother whom he had not seen for six years, and then he would learn he had been dead some months.

Frank had been a problem. Dickens found it difficult to settle him in any profession. The boy had been sent to Germany to learn the language, and from there he had written to his father:

"Dear papa, I write to tell you that I have given up all thoughts of being a doctor. My conviction that I shall never get over my stammering is the cause; all professions are barred against me. The only thing I should like to be is a gentleman-farmer, either at the Cape, in Canada, or Australia. With my passage paid, fifteen pounds, a horse, and a rifle, I could go two or three hundred miles up country, sow grain, buy cattle, and in time be very comfortable." His father's comments on this suggestion were: "I perceived that the first consequence of the fifteen pounds would be that he would be robbed of it – of the horse, that it would throw him – and of the rifle, that it would blow his head off."

So Frank was brought home; an unsuccessful attempt was made to find him a post in the Foreign Office, and it was proposed to make him a partner with his brother, Charley, who was trying to set up in business as a merchant. When this did not work out, Dickens took him into the office of *All the Year Round* where he proved to be of little help. So, finally, he obtained an appointment in the Bengal Mounted Police and sailed away. By January 1864, two sons had gone to India.

Charley Dickens had been adopted as Godson by Miss Coutts who generously paid for him to go to Eton. But, as his father noted, he lacked "continuous energy" and "a habit of perseverance", and had not proved a very able scholar. On leaving school he had been to Germany to learn the language, then to China to learn the tea trade, but showed no signs of making a success at anything. In 1861 he had married his childhood sweetheart, Bessie Evans, the daughter of Frederick Evans of the publishing firm, Bradbury and Evans. As Dickens had quarrelled with the firm over matters concerning his separation, he was not in favour of the match. He refused to attend the wedding, and even let his friends know that it was his "earnest hope" they would not "enter Mr. Evans's house on that occasion". Happily, Dickens did not alienate his son and daughter-in-law. Their child, Mary Angela, became a frequent visitor to Gad's Hill, and later in life recorded her recollections of the man she had called "Venerables".

Sydney seems always to have known that what he wanted to do in life was to be a sailor. A very small boy, he was quite a favourite with his father who was delighted when he passed out as a naval cadet. On 24th September 1860, Sydney ("the little Admiral", Dickens dubbed him) joined his training ship. His father went down to Portsmouth to see him off, look over the ship, and give him a gold sovereign.

"There is no denying," wrote Dickens, "that he looks very small aboard a great ship, and that a boy must have a strong and decided speciality for the sea to take to such a life." Later Sydney was posted to HMS Orlando and was commended as "a highly intelligent and promising young officer". In 1867 he was promoted Lieutenant. But Sydney was also to prove a great disappointment by running deeply into debt. At first his father paid his bills and gave him stern warnings against the folly of extravagant expenditure. But the same thing happened again and again, until, with a heavy heart, Dickens forbade him to come to Gad's Hill when next he landed in England.

Alfred had been to school in Boulogne and hoped to join the army. Unfortunately he failed to qualify for entry into the engineers or the artillery, so he began to think – as Frank had done – that perhaps he might make a doctor. Eventually he followed in the wake of his eldest brother and joined a China House in the City. His father felt he had an aptitude for business and might do well in Australia if he could gain mercantile employment with a good firm. So, armed with letters of introduction, Alfred embarked for Melbourne, and did indeed gradually make a career there. But he too was a spendthrift, and left a pile of unpaid bills behind him. His father was greatly saddened to discover this further evidence of extravagant expenditure by his children. Alfred had bought silk scarves, kid gloves, several suits, umbrellas – even a bottle of scent – and not paid for any.

Henry (or Harry), the next to youngest, was the only one to show any real academic ability. He had been at school in Boulogne with Alfred, but in 1860 was placed in Rochester Grammar School with his younger brother, Edward (the Plorn), who had hitherto been at home. He later went to a school in Wimbledon and from there, in October 1868, to Trinity Hall, Cambridge.

Edward (the Plorn) was his father's favourite, but he was a shy boy who could be bullied. Although he followed Harry to Wimbledon, he found such a large school confusing and asked to be placed in some smaller establishment. He was therefore transferred to Tunbridge Wells and studied under Mr. Sawyer, a clergyman. He had little power of perseverance, no "continuity of purpose" (his father said), and showed little promise of being a success in any profession. Dickens, finding that Alfred was managing to survive in Australia, conceived the idea that Plorn would 'take better to the Bush than to Books' and began to train him for such a life. He was taught various manual skills, and arrangements were made for him and join his brother.

The decision was a costly one for Dickens. He really loved Plorn, and to part with him was a tremendous sacrifice. He gave the boy a letter on the day of his departure:

"My Dearest Plorn, I write this note today because your going away is much upon my mind, and because I want you to have a few parting words from me to think of now and then at quiet times. I need not tell you that I love you dearly, and am very very sorry in my heart to part with you."

Plorn wept in the railway carriage as he journeyed from Higham, but his father, whom he met at Paddington, broke down in tears in public and was dreadfully upset. After the boy had gone, Dickens wrote to Charles Fechter: "Poor Plorn is gone to Australia. It was a hard parting at the last. He seemed to me to become once more my youngest and favourite little child as the day drew near, and I don't think I could have been so shaken."

Unfortunately, Plorn was not to settle down in Australia as easily as Dickens had hoped. He soon showed signs of wanting to come home.

"He seems to have been born without a groove," wrote Dickens in one of the last letters of his life. "What is curious to me is that he is very sensible, and yet does not seem to understand that he has qualified himself for no public examinations in the old country, and could not possibly hold his own against any competitor for anything to which I could get him nominated."

However, Plorn never returned to England.

Dickens reading to his daughters outside the front of Gad's Hill Place. Katey is standing and Mamie is kneeling.

Charles Dickens and his dog, Turk.
"A beautiful mastiff, with large, solemn, brown eyes. He was devoted to his Master,
who loved the dear beast." – *Mamie Dickens.*

Above: Dickens with members of his family and friends at Gad's Hill. *Men standing*: Wilkie Collins, C. A. Collins, C. Dickens Junr., Hamilton Hume. *Ladies*: Mrs C. Dickens Junr., the novelist's daughters, Mamie and Katey, and Miss Georgina Hogarth. *Men on lawn*: Fechter and Charles Dickens.

Left: Grave of the pet canary, Dick, in the garden of Gad's Hill.

Gad's Hill Place from the front lawn showing the drive and the roof to the right beneath which there were two bachelor's bedrooms and below them again, the servants' hall.

CHAPTER 5

Memorable Occasions

1 THE VISIT OF HANS CHRISTIAN ANDERSEN *June/July 1857*

Dickens first met Hans Christian Andersen, the Danish writer of fairy stories, at the home of Lady Blessington. He invited him to stay at Devonshire Terrace, but events made this impossible. Instead, when the family were staying at Broadstairs in the summer of 1847, Andersen was entertained to dinner. On the next day, Dickens accompanied him to Ramsgate and saw him safely aboard the packet for Ostend. Later that year he wrote to Andersen in Denmark: "come again to England soon!" Ten years later, Andersen accepted Dickens' invitation and came ostensibly to spend a fortnight at Gad's Hill. Dickens explained:

"We shall not be at home here in London itself after the first week of June, but we shall be at a little country house I have, only twenty-seven miles away. It is on a line of railroad, and within an hour and a half of London, in a very beautiful part of Kent. You shall have a pleasant room there with a charming view, and shall live as quietly and wholesomely as in Copenhagen. If you should want, at any time while you are with us, to pass the night in London, this house [i.e. Tavistock House where Dickens was then residing and writing from] from the roof to the cellar, will be at your disposal. . . . The two little girls you saw at Broadstairs, when you left England, are young women now, and my eldest boy is more than twenty years old. But we have children of all sizes and they all love you. You will find yourself in a house full of admiring and affectionate friends, varying from three feet high to five feet nine . . ."

Andersen arrived on 11th June. He was not met by his host, nor even by the groom and basket phaeton. But the stationmaster had been told to expect him and he kindly took Andersen's luggage on his back and carried it the mile and a half, up-hill, to the house. Dickens received him cordially, and invited him to have breakfast (called Brackfest, by

Andersen) with himself and Catherine. Afterwards they walked together, chatting, in the garden.

Andersen described his first impressions to his 'dear sisterly friend, Miss Henrietta Wulff':

"My reception was warm; Dickens took me in his arms; later his wife and children came. I was given a charming room and can from my window look down over Higham to the Thames, which swarms with ships. Dickens has aged somewhat and has a beard. . . . Mrs. Dickens I find this time beautiful, and the eldest daughter Mary takes after her, the second, Kate, has on the one hand quite Dickens' face, as you know it in his portrait; there are three sons over in Boulogne and four in this house; the youngest Edward Lytton Bulwer Dickens, appears to be five years old. All the children are named after writers. The eldest is called Charles Dickens; the second, Walter Landor (he is leaving in four weeks for Calcutta, where he shall become an officer, and will stay seven years away); then come the sons in Boulogne, Francis Jeffrey, Alfred Tennyson, Sydney Smith, and here at home the two youngest, Henry Fielding and Edward Bulwer. Of them all the little Henry was the first to show kindness to me."

Andersen went on to give a picture of family life at Gad's (as he saw it).

"The family life seems so harmonious, and a young Miss Hogarth [she was thirty that year], who has been living in this house for many years, pours tea and coffee, plays with the young Misses Dickens and seems to be a most kind and cultured lady. Dickens himself is like the best in his books – affectionate, lively, cheerful and cordial. Him I understand the best as far as speaking goes, and now – exactly eight days since I came – he says that I am making surprising progress in speaking English; every hour it is better, but then I speak without fear, and even the little ones begin to understand me. On Sunday I went with Dickens, Miss Hogarth, Walter and Henry to church. It was a long service, and we had to walk over half a Danish mile there and back again. The minister I did not understand at all, but did on the other hand the hymns."

The morning after his arrival, Andersen rather upset the elder Dickens boys. He not only expected to be waited on in bed and have his clothes brought to him by a maid, but he was incapable of shaving himself. He therefore sent for Charley Dickens and evidently demanded that Charley be his barber. No wonder that Harry in his *Recollections* years later spoke of "the intense indignation of the boys". Probably their own plans for the day were spoiled because Charley had to drive Andersen to a village about three miles away where it was hoped to find a barber, and this might well have been a futile journey. On the Friday however, he found a barber in "Roschester" where he had been driven with Mrs. Dickens, Georgina, Miss Burdett-Coutts and her companion, Hannah Brown. While he was there, as he recorded in *A Visit to Charles Dickens*:

"I strolled about in Rochester, which has been made the scene of several incidents in Pickwick. . . . I heard a Scotch bagpipe here; an old Scot wearing a kilt too short to cover his bare knees, managed the instrument; two small boys, dressed like the old man, walked on their hands and played other pranks, while a little sister of theirs danced up and down the pavement, swinging her kilt and singing. It looked quite pitiable."

Andersen amused the family considerably by his skill in cutting out figures and patterns from sheets of paper. He so impressed the children by his talent in using scissors in this way that when they came to write their memoirs years later they made a special point of mentioning it.

On the Saturday after his arrival he went with Catherine, Georgina, and Plorn to explore the countryside around Gad's Hill. He was not, like Dickens, a great walker, and the Monument to which he believed he had led the Dickenses for the first time was only a very short distance away. In his diary, Andersen recorded how Plorn had "held my hand and danced round me, asking about every imaginable thing and what it might be called in Danish, telling me what it was in English." Then after dinner, Miss Coutts kindly invited him to drive with her on the following Tuesday and spend the night at her house. Walter was to accompany him.

In the meantime, there was church attendance at Higham on Sunday. That would be St. Mary's Church where the Rev. Joseph Hindle (the late occupant of Gad's Hill Place) was the incumbent. There was no nearer church at that time, St. John's not being consecrated until 1862. Poor Andersen was "sorely tired" at having to walk back, and was not finding the June weather what he had expected; a cold wind was blowing from the east.

There were compensations, however. Forster and his wife came to dinner on Sunday evening. On Monday Dickens took him to see London, but as they had to leave the house early to catch the train there was no time to get into Rochester and visit the barber. So, according to his diary, "the whole day I went with a great growth of beard." This must have been embarrassing because it was a full day – calling at Tavistock House ('Davistockhouse' Andersen spelt it), driving to Sydenham where the Crystal Palace had been re-erected to attend a performance of *The Messiah*, and then returning to London to a performance at the Lyceum. At the end of the day, he was completely exhausted. The next morning after spending the night at Tavistock House, he walked arm in arm with Dickens to the office of *Household Words* and from thence on a busy round of calls. At six in the evening, he and Walter set out for Miss Coutts' house in Piccadilly. He noted that "she must be fabulously wealthy, with lodge keeper, footman in princely livery, carpeted staircases." He, the son of a cobbler and a washerwoman, found himself in the finest bedroom he had ever had "with a bathroom and privy, a fire in the fireplace . . . fine paintings and statues below." He found Miss Coutts easy to get on with, but was overawed by the servants.

So the visit went on, alternating between Gad's Hill and London. Dickens was busy with the work involved in raising money for Douglas Jerrold's widow, and as a result, others in the family had to amuse their guest. They did not always do it very well. Thus, on Monday 22nd June, Charley with two of his friends drove to town, and, as Andersen recorded: "Miss Hogarth said there would be room enough for me, since they would take the larger of the two carriages. I therefore accompanied them, but that was not what Charles wished, I came to understand very well; he was far from agreeable, and I returned in very bad humour, which I could not conceal. This is the first disagreeable day in England."

When Dickens was there, Andersen was perfectly happy, but he found the Dickens children resented him. He was happier with the Bentley family with whom he stayed for short periods. The weather while he was in England varied from very hot to very cold for the time of year. When Bentley took him to see the Queen distributing medals to her Crimean heroes, Andersen almost fainted from the heat, but he was complaining of the cold in the first week of July.

Returning to Gad's Hill after spending the night of 26th June at Bentley's, he was annoyed when he arrived at Higham station by finding Walter Dickens and one of the Evans boys ignoring him. They had been on the train from Gravesend, but when they alighted "neither of them showed any interest or attention in helping me by taking a little of my luggage; they walked ahead. . . . After dinner, tired; read the *Athenaeum*, upset; fell asleep, and was called at 8 o'clock for tea; I was very heavy in the head, tired and confused, had the feeling that no-one sympathised with me, so I told Mrs. Dickens and Miss Hogarth that I was very tired, and went to bed at 9 o'clock."

It was not only the people around him who were unsympathetic; the press (the *Athenaeum*) was severely critical of his new book *To Be, or Not to Be?* and Andersen took their strictures very much to heart. When Dickens returned home on 28th June he did his utmost to persuade his guest to disregard what the journals were saying. "Never allow yourself to be upset by the papers, they are forgotten in a week, and your book stands and lives." Dickens and Andersen went out for a stroll that evening and as they went, Dickens wrote with his foot in the sand "That is criticism," he said. Then he wiped it out. "And so it is gone." At dinner, someone asked Andersen how long he expected to remain in England. He did not record his exact reply, except that he added: "Long for Mr Dickens, short for me."

On Monday 29th June, Andersen came up to London Bridge station with Dickens and others of the family. Somehow he got parted from the others and decided to take a cab to Tavistock House. "The coachman drove me through such a poor quarter that I thought he meant me ill, but I came home safely. Miss Hogarth is not at all attentive, nor are the sons; there is altogether a great difference between the whole family and Dickens and his wife."

Dickens reported this incident to Miss Coutts saying: "We are suffering a good deal from Andersen" and when Andersen had at last gone home, he reported it more fully, and with typical exaggerations to William Jerdan:

"Whenever he got to London, he got into wild entanglements of cabs and Sherry, and never seemed to get out of them again until he came back here, and cut out paper into all sorts of patterns, and gathered the strangest little nosegays in the woods. His unintelligible vocabulary was marvellous. In French or Italian, he was the Peter the Wild Boy; in English, the Deaf and Dumb Asylum. My eldest boy swears that the ear of man cannot recognise his German; and his translatress declares to Bentley that he can't speak Danish! One day he came home to Tavistock House, apparently suffering from corns that had ripened in two hours. It turned out that a cab driver had brought him from the

City, by way of the new unfinished thoroughfare through Clerkenwell. Satisfied that the cabman was bent on robbery and murder, he had put his watch and money into his boots – together with a Bradshaw, a pocket-book, a pair of scissors, a penknife, a book or two, a few letters of introduction, and some other miscellaneous property."

He seemed to get on very well with Catherine, with whom he went to the Lyceum Theatre once or twice, and on 11th July to see a performance of *The Frozen Deep*, when Dickens' portrayal of Richard Wardour greatly impressed him. The following day he accompanied Dickens to Albert Smith's house at Welham Green. The entire company of *The Frozen Deep* were there to enjoy a splendid party, and it was then that the photograph of the company was taken. Andersen was displeased, however, with Walter Dickens' behaviour, and the entry in his diary contains the unamplified remark: "Young Walter Dickens silly!"

Nor did other young members of the family escape his criticism. "My little friend, (the musical genius) appeared casual and unfriendly towards me." This possibly refers to Harry, but the Dickens children were compared unfavourably with the young Bentleys, who, he confided to his diary, were "extremely kind, more sociable and sympathetic than Dickens' children."

The day before Andersen was due to leave was extremely hot. He was driven to Strood with Catherine and visited his barber again for a shave. Returning to Gad's Hill, he found a game of cricket in progress, several friends of the family taking part (but not Dickens who had a swollen face). In the course of the match, Mrs. Francis Carr Beard was unfortunately hit on the face by a ball, and left with a black eye.

On the following day, Dickens drove his visitor to Maidstone and saw him on the train to Folkestone where he was to catch the boat for France. The family was greatly relieved to see him go, and Dickens signified this by placing a placard on the dressing-table Andersen had used: "Hans Andersen slept in this room for five weeks which seemed to the family ages."

2 KATEY'S WEDDING   *17th July 1860*

After Dickens had separated from his wife (in May 1858, a year after Andersen's visit), life at Gad's Hill changed. Charley went to live with his mother and then went off to Hong Kong "to buy tea", the two girls remained at home, Walter was in India, Frank was preparing for a business career, and the younger boys were at school. But there was an uneasy tension between Dickens and his second daughter, Katey, and perhaps between Georgina and Katey. This followed Katey's siding with her mother over the separation. Her father, she said later, had been like a madman at that time. She told Gladys Storey that for two years her father would hardly speak to her because she refused to stop visiting her mother. The atmosphere in the house became so dreadful that she looked for an avenue of escape, and finally she saw the possibility of this in marriage.

There are doubts whether she was ever in love with Charles Allston Collins, but when he proposed to her she accepted. He was the brother of Dickens' friend and colleague, Wilkie Collins. Twelve years older than Katey, he was tall, pale, and red-headed (as Katey was too). He had gained some repute as a painter, was a member of the Pre-Raphaelite Brotherhood, and a colleague of Burne-Jones, Millais and Holman Hunt. As a writer he had contributed to Dickens' *All the Year Round* and produced one or two books. He was a man with some talent.

Dickens was not over-enthusiastic about this match. For one thing, he was not too friendly towards the Pre-Raphaelites, and his criticism in 1850 of Millais' *Christ in the Carpenter's Shop* had been violent to the verge of hysteria. It was a wonder that he was ever reconciled to Millais in later years. But Dickens was aware of Collins' delicate health, and feared that if Katey married him, she would be left a young widow in the not too distant future. Katey, however, was a strong-willed girl. 'Lucifer Box', her father had nicknamed her, and as she was determined on her course, the wedding plans went ahead.

Dickens busied himself with the arrangements, writing to the Rev. Joseph Hindle who would conduct the service to acquaint him with every detail.

"We arrange to be at the church at 20 minutes past 11 on Tuesday forenoon. The railway people have arranged to bring down three or four of our intimate friends, so that they shall arrive at Higham at five minutes past 11. I will have a carriage waiting for them there, and they shall be brought straight to the church."

Two days after the wedding he gave an account of it to the wife of his brother, Alfred, who was lying seriously ill in Manchester:

"Her marriage went off with the greatest success from first to last, and had no drawbacks whatever. We had tried to keep it quiet here, but the church was filled with people, and the energetic blacksmith of the village, had erected a triumphal arch in the court, and fired guns all night beforehand – to our great amazement, we not having the slightest idea what they meant. However, there were no annoyances to be grave about, so we laughed at them. We had so arranged for Katie's departure (for Dover) as that she should not have an hour of breakfast, so it was rapid, and no speechifying occurred, and they were gone in no time."

But there were one or two drawbacks which Dickens declined to mention. The chief one was the conspicuous absence of the bride's mother. There were tears, of course, amidst the congratulations. Katey could not help herself from bursting into tears as she bade farewell to her father and he held her in his arms. Nor could Mamie restrain herself. There was an awkward scene after the wedding breakfast when Dickens somehow got into an argument with Holman Hunt who was Collins' best man. The argument, which became embarrassingly heated for a few moments, was about a painting by David Roberts which Dickens had on his wall.

That evening when the visiting guests had departed and those staying in the house were resting, Mamie was going past her sister's bedroom when she became aware of someone within. She glanced round the door and discovered her father, on his knees by the bedside, sobbing into Katey's discarded bridal gown. When he saw her, he got to his feet. "But for me," he said in a choking voice, "Katey would not have left home."

He continued to be seriously concerned about Katey's marriage, and when writing about the wedding a month later, he described some of the amusing incidents before concluding: "There was no misery of any kind, not even speechifying, and the whole was a great success – SO FAR."

3 THE BONFIRE IN THE FIELD   *3rd September 1860*

Over the years Dickens had maintained a huge correspondence. Well over 13,000 letters written by him are known, and there must have been many more for which no evidence exists. Many of these were replies to letters from prominent persons in diverse spheres of life, not just fellow literary men and journalists, but politicians, men of science, actors and artists. Many, of course, were replies to friends, members of the family and employees, and many must have been of little or no importance. Dickens evidently kept most of the letters sent to him and by 1860 must have accumulated several thousand. No-one shall ever know what information these letters contained, what insights into Victorian life they might have afforded to later generations, what secrets were there, what revelations of character. No-one shall ever know – except in the few cases where correspondents had retained copies of their letters – because in September 1860, Dickens decided to destroy the entire collection.

"Yesterday," he wrote to W.H. Wills, "I burnt, in the field at Gad's Hill, the accumulated letters and papers of twenty years. They sent up a smoke like the Genie when he got out of the casket on the sea-shore; and as it was an exquisite day when I began, and rained very heavily when I finished, I suspect my correspondence of having overcast the face of the Heavens."

According to Gladys Storey, Katey and her two youngest brothers assisted in the work, feeding the flames with basketfuls of papers. Katey even begged her father to save some of the letters, but he was determined that they should all be destroyed. "We should always remember that letters are but ephemeral," he declared. "We must not be affected too much either by those which praise us or by others written in the heat of the moment." And when the last of the letters was cast on the fire, and the two boys were ready to roast onions in the hot ashes, he said with a sigh: "Would to God every letter I have ever written was on that pile."

In one respect, this bonfire was understandable. He was moving from one residence to another, and finally relinquishing Tavistock House. The very next day he handed over the keys to the new occupant. Henceforth Gad's Hill Place was to be his permanent home. It would seem natural therefore that he should clear out his cupboards and drawers at this time, as most ordinary people changing house would do. But he was no ordinary person, and it seems clear he was performing a symbolic break with the past. Most of these letters had been written in happier times, which he had no desire to be reminded of. They could each have an accusing finger pointing at him, so they had to be destroyed.

But he could not explain the real reason to other people, especially to those who knew what invaluable literary sources had been lost for posterity. He had to devise some plausible excuse and this, as he repeated to correspondents requesting access to documents he was possibly holding, was that he had been very shocked to see the way in which private letters had been misused. He had therefore decided not to retain any after they had been answered. However, when he related what he had done to the American Minister in France, and no doubt tried to justify himself by the excuse he had devised, the Minister, John Bigelow, exploded and told him he deserved to have been thrown on the bonfire himself.

4 DICKENS' RETURN HOME FROM AMERICA   *2nd May 1868*

Dickens left England for the United States on 9th November 1867 aboard the S.S. Cuba, to fulfil his undertaking to give eighty readings in American cities. He returned to Liverpool on 1st May 1868 aboard S.S. Russia. While in America he travelled extensively. From Boston he went south to New York and then shuttled between Baltimore and Philadelphia, returned north, made a long trip west to Buffalo and the Niagara Falls, and then confined himself to the New England area. As his manager, George Dolby wrote:

"Our operations in America were now confining themselves within narrow limits, and it was fortunate that it was so, for Mr. Dickens' health was becoming a graver source of anxiety every day. . . . A return of the snowstorms and severe frost brought a return of 'the true American' (as he used to call the catarrh), and also a return of the sleepless nights."

Although Dickens did not over-emphasise his ill-health to his family, he did not conceal that he was suffering from cough and catarrh, and no doubt they became extremely worried about him. But the voyage home, in spite of being stormy, proved to be a tonic. He told his friend the Hon. Mrs. Watson:

"The work in America has been so very hard, and the winter there has been so excessively severe, that I really have been very unwell for some months. But I had not been at sea three days on the passage home when I became myself again."

On landing in Liverpool, he was driven to the Adelphi Hotel, where he had stayed many times before. Any problems he and his party might have had with Customs had been circumvented by the Surveyor of Customs landing them and their baggage in the mail boat. So Dickens was able to enjoy a quiet dinner that evening before retiring to bed.

The next morning he journeyed by train to Euston Square where he parted with the men who had been his assistants throughout the tour. From Charing Cross Station he took the train for Gravesend. Having learned Higham villagers were planning to meet him at Higham station, with the intention of taking the horse out of his carriage and dragging him in triumph up to Gad's Hill Place, his family arranged for the carriage to go to Gravesend, the station before Higham.

Dickens described his arrival in a long letter to his American hostess, Mrs. Annie Fields:

"The two Newfoundland dogs, coming to meet me with the usual carriage and the usual driver, and beholding me coming in my usual dress out of the usual door, it struck me that their recollection of my having been absent for any unusual time was at once cancelled. They behaved (they are both young dogs) exactly in their usual manner; coming behind the basket phaeton as we trotted along, and lifting their heads to have their ears pulled – a special attention which they receive from no-one else. But when I drove into the stable-yard, Linda (the St. Bernard) was greatly excited; weeping profusely, and throwing herself on her back that she might caress my foot with her great fore-paws. Mamie's little dog, too, Mrs. Bouncer, barked in the greatest agitation on being called down and asked by Mamie, 'Who is this?' and tore round and round me, like the dog in the Faust outlines. You must know that all the farmers turned out on the road in their market-chaises to say, 'Welcome home, sir!' and that all the houses along the road were dressed with flags; and that our servants, to cut out the rest, had dressed this house so that every brick of it was hidden. They had asked Mamie's permission to 'ring the alarm-bell'(!) when master drove up, but Mamie, having some slight idea that that compliment might awaken master's sense of the ludicrous, had recommended bell-abstinence. But on Sunday, the village choir (which includes the bell-ringers) made amends. After some unusually brief pious reflection in the crowns of their hats at the end of the sermon, the ringers bolted out and rang like mad until I got home."

5 VISITS BY AMERICAN FRIENDS *July 1868 and June 1869*

Dickens was frequently in Longfellow's company while he was in Boston. He had dined at Longfellow's house, and had then given a dinner in return. Both occasions had been very pleasant; the two men greatly appreciated one another and the company included many distinguished Bostonians. At the dinner-party he gave, Dickens was feeling rather better in health than he had been for a while, and accordingly was in a particularly jovial mood. Dolby noted that "even the most dignified of the guests caught the infection and went in for the fun."

Longfellow was planning to visit England that summer with his daughter and brother-in-law, so Dickens arranged for them to make a brief stay at Gad's Hill. The weather that summer was not oscillating between extremes of heat and cold as it had been when Andersen came. This enabled the visitors to enjoy the special arrangements their host had made for their entertainment. Dolby, who with Mr. and Mrs. Charles Eliot Norton, Charles Kent and John Forster, was in the house-party, described these arrangements.

"Two post carriages, with postillions in the 'old red jacket of the old red royal Dover Road', were turned out, and the antiquities of Rochester and its castle having been visited, we drove to Blue Bell Hill (a favourite spot with Mr. Dickens); and when the time came for our return to London, the holiday had passed all too quickly."

Dolby also left an account of the way Dickens looked after the small details of this, and similar outings.   ·

"Ever mindful of the comfort and convenience of his guests, and knowing how much the happiness of the day depends on these, Mr. Dickens had a plan of his own in the conduct of these arrangements; and instead of entailing the labour, consequent on the carrying of the lunch-baskets to some picturesque and secluded spot, on certain individuals of the party, he arranged that everyone should carry his own lunch, and nobody else's. For this purpose he had a quantity of small baskets, in which were packed all the necessaries for the midday meal; and as nothing – not even the pepper, salt, mustard, and corkscrews – was ever forgotten, the petty worries and annoyances so common at picnics were avoided by his forethought."

A year later, Mr. and Mrs. James T. Fields arrived in England. Dickens had first met Fields (partner in the firm of Ticknor and Fields) during his trip to America in 1842, and when he arrived for his second visit, Fields had been one of the party aboard the Customs boat who went out to welcome him. Fields and his wife, Annie, were great admirers of Dickens. They had observed him at close quarters when he had stayed in Boston; they had accompanied him on visits to other friends, and entertained him to dinner. Annie Fields, a shrewd and articulate lady, later recorded her insights into the "inner" Dickens which lay underneath the hearty genial exterior.

Dickens met his visitors in London where he was staying at St. James' Hotel, 77 Piccadilly. He took them to see the sights (what he always called "the lions") – Windsor Castle, Richmond, St. Paul's. He took Fields out with the police on two nights "to have a glimpse of the darker side of London life". On one of these expeditions they visited the opium-den which was to figure in the first chapter of *Edwin Drood*. After this sojourn in the capital, the Fields went to Gad's Hill on 2nd June where a large house-party was gathered, several guests being accommodated across the road at the Sir John Falstaff.

Barely a month had passed since Dickens' breakdown at Preston when his doctor had ordered the cancellation of the reading tour, but already he seemed to have recovered. When Dolby met him at Higham station to join the American party, he found "all traces of his illness had disappeared. In his light suit of clothes and round hat, carried jauntily on the side of his head, he looked the picture of health."

Dolby left a very full account of this visit during which Dickens repeated the excursions:

"One of the most delightful days . . . was occupied by a drive from Gad's Hill to Canterbury, a distance of twenty-nine miles, over the old Dover Road, through Rochester, Chatham, Sittingbourne, and Faversham. We were to make an early start. . . . Two post carriages were turned out with postillions in the red jackets of the old Royal Dover Road, buckskin breeches, and top-boots into the bargain. . . . I can see now the hampers and wine baskets blocking the steps of the house before they were packed in the carriages. . . . We drove into Canterbury in the early afternoon, just as the bells of the Cathedral were ringing for afternoon service. . . . Being in Canterbury Cathedral, Mr. Dickens considered it necessary to show his friends the many objects of interest there; and after he had politely but speedily got rid of a tedious verger who wanted to lead the way, he played the part of cicerone himself in the most genial and learned style in the world."

There were other outings and festivities in honour of the American guests, concluding with "a grand dinner-party in the evening with a reception afterwards, which many friends in the neighbourhood attended. The furniture had been removed from the drawing-room during dinner for the dance, and it was not until the morning light peeped in at the windows that the guests separated."

Mrs. Field greatly enjoyed her stay and the brilliant company. "Wonderful," she observed later, "the flow of spirits Charles Dickens has *for a sad man*."

CHAPTER 6

Anecdotes, Snippets, and the Gad's Hill Gazette

Dickens' dogs used to get a good meal every day. The cook prepared five plates for them ready to be taken out into the yard, one plate for each dog, including Mamie's Pomeranian, Mrs. Bouncer. The youngest dog, Bumble, was a Newfoundland, the son of Don, another of Dickens' dogs. One day Bumble sneaked unobserved into the kitchen after the cook had just prepared the platefuls and while she was attending to other duties. Seeing so much food, Bumble could not restrain himself. He ate the lot, and then, his stomach distended, he fainted away. The cook came back to find an apparently dead dog, and five empty plates. Fortunately, Bumble suffered no harm. He was taken outside and put under the pump where he revived.

*

Dickens was very keen on a daily shower-bath, and he complained if a shower was not "sharp". He had one installed in Gad's Hill Place, but when he was away he would go to the public baths. When he went to Brighton, for instance, he set out to the baths early in the morning before breakfast. "They kept me waiting longer than I thought reasonable," he complained, but when he went to order a man in the passage, whom he presumed to be the attendant, to go and see about it, the man turned out to be another intending bather, and was in fact a very old friend of Dickens' – John Hullah, the composer of the music for Dickens' operetta, *The Village Coquettes*.

*

One evening in October 1860, strange rumours came to Gad's Hill Place. Someone said there was a ghost up at Larkins' monument, and the story was evidently supported with such convincing detail that Dickens felt uneasy. Eight-year-old Plorn was quite terrified, but his

father was apprehensive that the servants, being credulously super-
stitious, would quit the house if the rumour could not be scotched
quickly. Of his older boys, only Frank was at home, but staying with
them was the son of a Scottish sheriff, Andrew Gordon, who was rather
sweet on Katey. So Dickens enlisted both of them as helpers.

"Time, nine o'clock," Dickens recorded. "Village talk and credulity
amazing. I armed the two boys with a short stick apiece, and shouldered
my double-barrelled gun, well loaded with shot. 'Now observe,' says I to
the domestics, 'if anybody is playing tricks and has got a head, I'll blow
it off.' Immense impression. New groom evidently convinced that he
has entered the service of a bloodthirsty demon. We ascend to the
monument. Stop at the gate. Moon is rising. Heavy shadows. 'Now,
look out!' (from the blood thirsty demon, in a loud distinct voice). 'If the
ghost is here and I see him, so help me God I'll fire at him!' Suddenly,
as we enter the field, a most extraordinary noise responds – terrific noise
– human noise – and yet superhuman noise. B.T.D. brings piece to
shoulder. 'Did you hear that, pa?' asked Frank. 'I did', says I. Noise
repeated – portentous, derisive, dull, dismal, damnable. We advance
towards the sound. Something white come lumbering through the
darkness. An asthmatic sheep!"

*

Harry Dickens recorded the following incident:

"One summer night, when the heat was intense, the company – and
there were several of us that evening – were seated in the hall after
dinner with both doors, in front and at the back, thrown wide open;
when suddenly, a bat flew into the hall and, as is the wont of bats, flew
wildly high and low, backwards and forwards, causing panic amongst
all assembled. There was a rush for protection in the rooms leading out
of the hall. The bat at last, in despair, took refuge in a recess in the
ceiling which could not be reached from the floor; and there it remained
– nothing would induce it to budge. Something had to be done –
somebody must have the courage to do what was necessary to dislodge
it. It was then that my father came to the rescue. He called for the library
ladder and a stick, and advanced to the attack. Suddenly it struck him
that his head was uncovered and he had misgivings lest the bat might
get mixed up with his hair. No adequate protection being at hand, he
called for a hip-bath – of all unlikely things! With this protection on his
head, like a new kind of helmet, he put his foot upon the ladder, and

Dickens preparing to drive the basket phaeton with the three ladies of Gad's Hill accompanying him. Marsh the stableman is holding the pony's head. One of the dogs can be seen lying down at the other side of the wheel.

Katey Dickens, his younger daughter, photographed on the steps of Gad's Hill Place.

Katey reading to Dickens' grand-daughter, Mary Angela Dickens, known as Mekitty.

Above left: Mrs Annie Fields who had been Dickens' hostess during his American tour, left an interesting account of her impressions of Dickens for whom she had the greatest admiration while not being blind to his faults.

Above: James T. Fields, partner in the publishing firm of Ticknor and Fields of Boston. He and his wife visited Dickens in 1869 and Dickens arranged several outings for them to Canterbury and elsewhere.

Left: Hans Christian Andersen who stayed at Gad's Hill Place in 1857.

Dickens reading on the back lawn of Gad's Hill Place. It is supposed that the book was Carlyle's *French Revolution.*

Sofa on which Dickens lay after his stroke on 8th June 1870 and on which he died the following day. Now in the Birthplace Museum, Portsmouth.

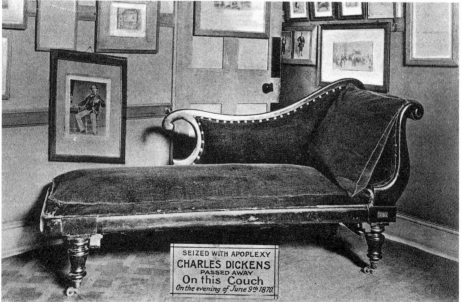

SEIZED WITH APOPLEXY
CHARLES DICKENS
PASSED AWAY
On this Couch
On the evening of June 9th 1870

began to climb; but the bath, being but an unstable headpiece, began to wobble; as he mounted it wobbled still more and more, until the contest reduced itself into one not of between himself and the bat, but between the bath and himself. It was at this critical time that the ridiculous side of the situation suddenly struck him and he at once became convulsed with laughter, until at last the bath fell down with a crash and my father fell back on the floor quite overcome, and the attack was at an end; but luckily the bat, startled no doubt by the unusual noise below him, solved the difficulty by retreating from the hiding-place and flying out into the night."

*

Dickens was photographed driving the basket phaeton (sometimes referred to merely as "the basket") and apparently drove one or other of the carriages quite frequently when he was at home. But it seems that Mamie was the keenest driver of the family. Her father wrote to De Cerjat:

"You don't say, my dear Cerjat, when you are coming to England! ... Say you are coming, and you shall be the first man turned over by it [the new jaunting-car]; somebody must be (for my daughter Mary drives anything that can be harnessed, and I know of no English horse that would understand a jaunting-car coming down a Kentish hill), and you shall be that somebody if you will. They turned the basket-phaeton over, last summer, in a bye-road, Mary and the other two – and had to get it up again; which they did, and came home as if nothing had happened."

A little more than a year after this accident, in October 1860, Mary had ridden out to Milton on the eastern outskirts of Gravesend by the river, about 4 miles from Gad's Hill. Suddenly her horse, Boy, went down and threw her. Her riding habit was badly torn, and she suffered a very nasty cut just above the knee which prevented her from walking for some weeks. Evidently messengers were sent to appraise the household of the accident, and when the carriage came to take her home she was discovered being looked after in a public house, "wonderfully taken care of" as her father described it.

The next February, Dickens took a furnished house in Regent's Park, and during the family's absence the servants at Gad's Hill disported themselves on the horses. The weather had, in fact, been very bad and everywhere frozen, then there was a thaw.

"Since then," wrote Dickens, "we have had a small visitation of the plague of servants; the cook (in a riding-habit) and the groom (in a dress coat and jewels) having mounted Mary's horse and mine . . . and scoured the neighbouring country at a rattling pace. And when I went home last Saturday, I innocently wondered how the horses came to be out of condition, and gravely consulted the said groom on the subject, who gave it as his opinion 'which they wanted reg'lar work'."

It would seem, therefore, that Dickens not only drove the carriages, but occasionally saddled a horse and went riding. His statement after the Staplehurst railway accident that he had been too shaken to continue driving and could not contemplate riding any more, would seem to confirm this.

*

Another activity by the owner of Gad's Hill Place which has received little attention, is that of rowing. In August 1859, Dickens apologised for not having written to Wilkie Collins about the choice of a title for his new novel *The Woman in White*, his excuse being that:

"I was tempted out on the Medway for two summer days (rowed 20 miles at a stretch on one of them), and so slided back in the *Tale of Two Cities*, and have since been doggedly at it. . . . The Medway I have discovered to be so surprisingly beautiful, that next year I hope to start a pretty boat, and give you aquatic relaxation. Immense enthusiasm and approval have been awakened in Gad's Hill by this new idea: oak outside, white within, touch of blue here and there, pink striped awning, Dick at the Prow, and Wilkie at the Helm, etc., etc., etc. (Mary has been found to have a natural genius for steering.)"

*

When Dickens took his American visitors to Canterbury, he stopped on the way in Rochester High Street to call at one of the shops. Today, descendants of some of those shopkeepers still cherish family recollections of him. On this occasion, a small crowd collected, attracted in all probability by the sight of red-jacketed postillions and the old-fashioned post-chaises which had not been seen there for some years. Dolby, who was in one of the carriages, noted that:

"it seemed to be pretty generally known amongst them that Dickens was of the party, and we got a good deal of fun out of the mistake made by a man in the crowd, who pointed up at Mr. James T. Fields and called out, 'That's Dickens!' Poor Fields was in great confusion, especially when Mr. Dickens, to complete the deception, handed up a small parcel to him, with the request, 'Here you are, Dickens, take charge of this for me.'"

*

Dolby had another anecdote about Fields, who had made a brief visit to the Continent after his stay at Gad's Hill. On his return he was found to have developed "a collector's mania for bric-a-brac and old furniture". Dickens humoured him in this new-found interest by accompanying him on several afternoons around London dealers, and did his best to deter him from buying numerous old things at vastly inflated prices. Eventually, hoping to cure his friend of this mania, Dickens wrote him the following letter:

"There is a chair (without a bottom) at a shop near the office which I think would suit you. It cannot stand of itself, but will *almost* seat somebody, if you put it in a corner, and prop one leg up with two wedges, and cut another leg off. The proprietor asks £20, but says he admires literature and would take £18. He is of *republican* principles, and I think would take £17.19s, from a cousin; shall I secure this prize? It is very old and wormy, and it is related, without proof, that on one occasion Washington declined to sit down on it."

*

Dickens did not like to be called 'Grandfather', and was rather amazed that he had attained that status. Instead, he asked to be called 'Venerables', and this was the name by which he was known to little 'Mekitty' (Mary Angela, daughter of Charley). She later achieved some success as a novelist, and left the following recollections.

"Four distinct pictures of my grandfather hold their places in my memory, and oddly enough, each one of the four reflects more or less definitely a different phase in his many-sided character. In the first I see the dining-room at Gad's Hill, and a large dinner-party in progress. It is very gay and very glittering, many flowers, much glass, much silver . . . and everyone is in a great good humour. I think it must be Christmas Day, as I can imagine no other reason for the presence on the scene of my little brother and myself. My little brother – a mere mite, a great favourite and innocent of the 'seen and not heard' adage – said or did something which caught my grandfather's attention. I can see the figure at the head of the table standing with his glass in his hand, alert, laughing, full of the zest of the moment, and pausing for an instant to say something to the little boy – something which I probably did not understand, and certainly do not remember – which was received with peals of laughter, in which the child joined gleefully without the faintest idea what it was all about! Here then is the social Charles Dickens, the delightful companion whose friends invariably forgot that he had ever written anything, so great was the charm of his capacity for enjoyment, so great was his gift for causing those about him to enjoy. He talked well, because he was so full of spirit, and so keenly observant, and because his sense of humour was wholly irrepressible. But he never talked otherwise than naturally and unaffectedly, and he was never bookish. . . . In my second picture . . . my grandfather is standing in front of a red and roaring fire – again in the dining-room at Gad's Hill. There is a very high and a very narrow mantelpiece, and he is framed, so to speak, against the background of cheery flame. On either side of the fireplace is a window, through which the garden, covered with snow, can be seen. My grandfather, handsome, alert, but for the moment a little at a loss, looks down at me. I, a very small girl in a pinafore look up at him. . . . I have been sent into the room alone, with the impression strong upon me that something tremendous is going to happen to me – my grandfather is going to give me a Christmas present himself. The present was one of the few children's Annuals of those days – the *Child's Prize*, and I do not doubt that my aunt had bought it, and had asked him to perform the ceremony of its bestowal. And my grandfather either was not in spirits that morning – let no one suppose that he alone among all geniuses never paid the penalty exacted by his gift – or else my preternatural solemnity seemed to demand a return in kind. So there we stood, the presentation being made, and I always wonder how the interview closed. It seems it might have gone on interminably. . . .

"On one of my visits to Gad's Hill, running about where I should not have been allowed to go, I fell over a saucepan of boiling water. Dinner was going on, and my nurse, frightened at the result of her short-comings, dared not disturb my aunt, and accordingly put me to bed, and told me not to cry. My aunt, coming to see me after dinner, instantly discovered my unhappy plight, but to my astonishment it was my grandfather who appeared at my bedside and 'made me better'. And through the unhappy days that followed – for I was badly scalded – the faith that he would always 'make me better' never left me. In the

course of those days he had to go to London, and my childish misery
was great . . . until 'Venerables' . . . came back. I can remember the joy
of hearing the pony carriage which brought him from the station drive
into the yard, and can see him, almost immediately afterwards, coming
into the room to me – a little invalid, waiting in perfect confidence to be
'made better!' . . .

"It was my father, I think, who was determined that I should be taken
to one of the last series of readings, and he naturally chose for me the
Christmas Carol. Curiously enough, I was not in the least elated at such
an unusual form of 'treat' – I think the necessity for being very good
must have been unduly impressed upon me! But I never went into the
St. James's Hall in after years without looking at the place where I sat on
that occasion, and feeling again the half-frightened expectation of I
knew not what, which I felt then. I see my grandfather now, as I saw him
then, standing at the little table, not 'Venerables' at all, but a terrible
and unknown personage, a long way off, quite unaware of my existence
and speaking in unknown voices. And I count among the most dreadful
moments of my childish existence the moment 'Venerables' cried."

*

Mekitty's father, Charles Dickens the Younger, also wrote down his
reminiscences of his father, and recalled his behaviour while busily
engaged on a novel:

"When he was writing one of his long stories and had become deeply
interested in the working-out of his plot and the evolution of his
characters, he lived, I am sure, two lives, one with us and one with his
fictitious people, and I am equally certain that the children of his brain
were much more real to him at times than we were. I have often and
often heard him complain that he could *not* get the people of his
imagination to do what he wanted, and that they would insist on
working out their histories in *their* way and not *his*. I can very well
remember his describing their flocking round his table in the quiet
hours of a summer morning when he was – an unusual circumstance
with him – at work very early, each one of them claiming and
demanding instant personal attention.

"At such times he would often fall to consider the matter in hand even
during his walks. There was no mistaking the silence into which he fell
on such occasions. It was not the silence only of a pause in conversation,

but the silence of engrossing thought, not, one felt, to be broken
or interrupted lightly. Many a mile have I walked with him thus
– he striding along with his regular four-miles-an-hour swing; his
eyes looking straight before him, his lips slightly working, as they
generally did when he sat thinking and writing; almost unconscious of
companionship, and keeping half a pace or so ahead. When he had
worked out what had come into his mind he would drop back again
into line – again, I am sure, almost unconsciously – and the conversation would be resumed, as if there had been no appreciable break or
interval at all."

*

Many people who lived in the neighbourhood of Gad's Hill have related
their recollection of Dickens out walking with his dogs. One man
recalled how "he held his head high up when he walked, and went at
great strides", another how he was always "theatrically dressed", and yet
another how he would hold his umbrella by the middle. Several people
remembered seeing him on Monday, 6th June, when for the last time
he walked to Rochester. One saw him leaning against the palings of
Restoration House, looking attentively at the building.

After Dickens' death, many local people recalled bits of information
which had some bearing on *The Mystery of Edwin Drood*. A Mr. Miles,
the Rochester Cathedral verger who might well have been the model for
Mr. Tope, believed that Dickens had based Durdles on a drunken old
German stonemason who, about thirty years previously, was always
prowling about "trying to pick up little bits of stone ornaments . . .
which he carried about in a cotton handkerchief." Mr Miles also
recalled that the room over the gatehouse which Dickens had allocated
to John Jasper had once been occupied, not by a cathedral choirmaster,
but by an organ-blower.

*

Charley Dickens recalled an interesting happening when he and his
father were both at Gad's Hill Place and Charley was working in the
library on some editorial job.

"Where he was I did not know, but, supposing him to be in the Swiss
chalêt over in the shrubbery across the road, I took advantage of having
the place to myself and went steadily on with my work. Presently I
heard a noise as if a tremendous row were going on outside, and as if

two people were engaged in a violent altercation or quarrel which threatened serious results to somebody. Ours being a country constantly infested with tramps, I looked upon the disturbance at first as merely one of the usual domestic incidents of tramp life arising out of some nomadic gentleman beating his wife up our lane, as was quite the common custom, and gave it hardly a moment's attention. Presently the noise came again, and yet again, worse than before, until I thought it really necessary to ascertain what was going on. Stepping out of the door on to the lawn at the back I soon discovered the cause of the disturbance. There, at the other end of the meadow, was my father, striding up and down, gesticulating wildly, and, in the character of Mr. Sikes, murdering Nancy with every circumstance of the most aggravated brutality. After dinner I told him what I had seen, and he read me the murder – it was rather a startler for an audience of one – and asked me what I thought of it. 'The finest thing I have ever heard,' was my verdict, 'but don't do it.'"

*

Gad's Hill Place was not always the most comfortable place in the world. In December 1860 "it was so intensely cold," said Dickens, "that in our warm dining-room on Christmas Day we could hardly sit at the table. In my study on that morning, long after a great fire of coal and wood had been lighted, the thermometer was I don't know where below freezing. The bath froze, and all the pipes froze, and remained in a stony state for five or six weeks. The water in the bedroom jugs froze, and blew up the crockery. The snow on the top of the house froze, and was imperfectly removed with axes. My beard froze as I walked about, and I couldn't detach my cravat and coat from it until I was thawed at the fire."

*

In order to keep the younger boys out of mischief, Dickens encouraged them in 1863 to begin a small weekly newspaper, the *Gad's Hill Gazette*. Alfred and Sydney were at home during this summer, and they were helped in the venture by their younger brothers, Harry and Plorn. They were given a little room as an office, complete with a bell to ring for their office-boy. The older boys soon tired of the venture and Harry and Plorn carried on with it for a while until Plorn, too, lost interest and all editorial duties fell to Harry.

The *Gazette* was first a mere hand-written issue, with a few copies in carbon. Later, however, W. H. Wills presented the editor with a manifold writer, and as the *Gazette* prospered he improved upon this by giving them a small printing press. This was not easy to handle because it required some type-setting skill, and Harry had to undergo a short period of training at a printing shop in London before the first printed edition of the paper could be published. The *Gazette* had quite a large circulation. There were eventually about a hundred subscribers paying twopence a copy, publication being confined to school holidays when the editor was available to gather the news, write the leading articles, solicit letters and other contributions, and set up the type.

The *Gazette* ran a lively correspondence page. There were grumbles, when the issues were produced by means of the manifold writer, that some of the copies were illegible. The editor made a spirited reply, pointing out the lack of funds to invest in a better mode of production, and he was stoutly defended in a letter from John Leech. The editor's father, too, joined in the correspondence column, writing letters under various fictitious names and replying to himself in the guise of other characters.

The *Gad's Hill Gazette* contained a lot of information about the various arrivals at and departures from the house. In the issue for 5th August 1865, for example, it was reported that Percy Fitzgerald, Esq. left on Tuesday 1st August, and Mr. & Mrs. Charles Collins (Katey and her husband), Charles Dickens, Miss Dickens (Mamie), and Miss Hogarth left on Saturday and returned the next morning at 1 o'clock a.m. Charles Dickens, Junior, arrived on Friday and left on the next day. Under the heading "Miscellaneous", the editor reported that the Gad's Hill party went to Knebworth (home of Bulwer Lytton) on Saturday morning to view the new houses built by The Guild of Literature and Art. A very handsome lunch was given by Sir E. B. Lytton Bart. in the course of which he, and C. Dickens Esq., delivered two brilliant speeches (spelled "speechs" by the editor). Dancing then followed, and the Gad's Hill party, who had spent a very pleasant day, returned late at night. Another paragraph informed readers that Linda, the dog, was much better.

Sports news occupied quite a high proportion of the *Gazette*'s space. One and half pages were devoted to the results of the Upper Higham versus Lower Higham cricket match on Friday, 28th July, which the latter team won by six wickets. The scores were not impressive. Harry

Dickens made three runs in the first innings and one run in the second. Charles Dickens, Junior, made a duck in each innings, and Plorn one run in each. Gouge was the best batsman on the Upper Higham side. He made five runs in the first, and nineteen in the second innings. Mr. Hindle (presumably the son of the rector) made a duck in the first innings, but achieved eleven runs in the second. They were no match for their opponents, however, who possessed a great batsman in one Barnes, who made a total of thirty-seven runs that day. The sports page concluded with a one-line entry in which the editor very modestly announced that "H. Dickens is the present champion at billiards".

After the summer issues, *Gazette* readers had to wait until Christmas for the next one, when the editor declared: "We are very glad to meet our subscribers again after such a long lapse of time, and we hope they will patronise us in the same kind and indulgent manner as they did last season." The main news was of the Christmas events:

"During the past week, Gad's Hill has resounded with the sounds of festivity and merriment. As is usually the case, the house has been filled with guests who have come to taste Mr. Dickens' hospitality. These consisted of Mr., Madame, and Master Fechter, Mr. and Mrs. Charles Collins, Mr., Mrs. and Master Charles Dickens, Junior, Mr. Morgan (who suddenly appeared on Christmas Day, having just returned from America), Mr. M. Stone, Mr. Chorley, and Mr. Dickenson. The latter gentleman has not yet entirely recovered from the effects of a most disastrous railway accident in which he was a sufferer, and had it not been for the courage and intrepidity of Mr. Dickens he would not now be spending his Christmas at Gad's Hill."

The editor then described how his father had pulled Mr. Dickenson from underneath a carriage where he had been lying unconscious and bleeding. The social report continued: "On Christmas Day, Mr., Mrs and Miss Malleson came to dinner. At about 9.0, an extempore dance began and was kept up till about 2 o'clock Tuesday morning. During the week billiards has been much resorted to." A report of the billiards contest shows that although Mr. Dickenson was the winner of the Great Handicap match on Christmas Day, he was not so good a player as Marcus Stone "(who however was so heavily weighted that he could not win)." The news ended with an advance notice: "On Saturday 30th a match is to be played between the Earl of Darnley and Mr. M. Stone."

*

The *Gad's Hill Gazette* continued to appear until its editor went up to Trinity Hall, Cambridge. Dickens was very proud of Harry's success in getting to the university. The lack of enterprise in his other sons had been a bitter disappointment to him. His disappointment lies behind the following incident related by Harry:

"In the year 1869, after I had been at college about a year, I was fortunate enough to gain one of the principal scholarships at Trinity Hall, Cambridge – not a great thing, only £50 a year; but I knew that this success, slight as it was, would give [my father] intense pleasure, so I went to meet him at Higham Station upon his arrival from London to tell him of it. As he got out of the train I told him the news. He said, 'Capital! capital!' – nothing more. Disappointed to find that he received the news apparently so lightly, I took my seat beside him in the pony carriage he was driving. Nothing more happened until we got half-way to Gad's Hill, when he broke down completely. Turning towards me with tears in his eyes and giving me a warm grip of the hand, he said, 'God bless you, my boy; God bless you!' That pressure of the hand I can feel now as distinctly as I felt it then, and it will remain as strong and real until the day of my death."

CHAPTER 7

Achievements at Gad's Hill

Little Dorrit was published in volume form on 30th May 1857; two days later the Dickens family moved into Gad's Hill Place for the first time. All of Dickens' works subsequent to *Little Dorrit* may therefore be counted as his achievements at the house. These include the novels *A Tale of Two Cities* (1859), *Great Expectations* (1860–61), *Our Mutual Friend* (1864–1865), and the unfinished *Mystery of Edwin Drood* (1870). There were also a number of minor works which will be detailed later.

It is not to be supposed, however, that Dickens wrote all, or even the greater part of these novels at Gad's Hill. One always imagines him seated in his chair at the library desk, or perched among the leafy branches in the upper room of the chalet, driving his shorn quill pen across sheets of pale blue paper. But in fact he did a great deal of his literary work away from home. Much of *A Tale of Two Cities* and *Great Expectations* was written at the office of *All the Year Round* in Wellington Street, London. We know from the statement in the Postscript that parts of *Our Mutual Friend* were written in France: "On Friday, the Ninth of June in the present year, Mr. and Mrs. Boffin (in their manuscript dress of receiving Mr. and Mrs. Lammle at breakfast) were on the South Eastern Railway with me, in a terribly destructive accident." This was when he was returning via Dover.

The idea for the plot of *A Tale of Two Cities* was no doubt suggested by that of Wilkie Collins' play *The Frozen Deep* in which Dickens had played the lead. He quickly set to work on this book because it was needed in the launch of his new journal *All the Year Round*. On 11th March 1859, a matter of weeks before the date of publication (30th April 1859) he told Forster: "This is to certify that I have got exactly the name for the story that is wanted; exactly what will fit the opening to a T. A TALE OF TWO CITIES."

In October 1860 he wrote to Forster about his next novel, also due to be serialised in his weekly magazine. "Last week, I got to work on a new story. . . . When I come down, I will bring you the first two or three weekly parts. The name is, GREAT EXPECTATIONS. I think a good name?"

Dickens spent a lot of time before actually beginning any of his later novels in thinking out the overall design and deciding on the theme, symbolism, characters and so on. He would be restless for weeks, pondering all these essential matters. When he came to write *Our Mutual Friend* he had more difficulty than ever in reconciling the various strands he wished to weave into the plot. In October 1863, he declared: "I am exceedingly anxious to begin my new book. I am bent upon getting to work at it." He said he needed to get back to Gad's Hill for five or six consecutive days in order to do so. A great deal of it, including the title, had already been settled in his mind, but, he said, "if I don't strike while the iron (meaning myself) is hot, I shall drift off again and have to go through all this uneasiness once more."

Dickens once again began to go through "the preliminary agonies of a new book" in October 1869. (October seems to have been the month for the 'quickenings' of these last novels.) He was soon at work on this one, *The Mystery of Edwin Drood*, and had completed most of the first two monthly numbers by the end of November. Although he probably did this at Gad's Hill, he must have written most of the remaining four instalments (all that were ever completed) at 5 Hyde Park Place, London, which he rented from January to May. He did, however, write the final pages in the chalet.

There is a thread running through these four "Gad's Hill" novels which has not received much attention. *They are all concerned with repentance*. This was not an entirely new theme for Dickens; Scrooge's repentance is the theme of *A Christmas Carol*, Mr. Dombey's repentance that of *Dombey and Son*, and young Martin's that of *Martin Chuzzlewit*. In the later novels repentance is treated in a variety of ways and more seriously. Sydney Carton's turning away from his life of dissipation and his redeeming himself by self-sacrifice begins the series. Throughout the novel the repetition and variation of the 'Restored to Life' leitmotif emphasises the repentance theme and suggests that Carton is 'restored to life' by losing his own. At the back of Dickens' mind must have been the gospel statement: "Whosoever shall lose his life . . . shall gain it."

Another penitent character is Pip in *Great Expectations*, who gradually comes to realise what a self-centred and condescending snob he has been since being 'made a gentleman', and so finally comes to confess to "Joe and Biddy both . . . that I was thankless . . . that I was ungenerous and unjust . . ."

In *Our Mutual Friend*, Bella comes to repent of her former longing for money, and her hatred of being poor. "We are degradingly poor, offensively poor, miserably poor, beastly poor!" Finally she comes to see she would rather be happy than rich. Other characters in this novel also come to repent, principally Eugene Wrayburn who, having been almost drowned, is 'born again' in his love for Lizzie, the waterman's daughter. And when he is induced to marry 'this lady', as Twemlow calls her, using the phrase in all sincerity, Podsnap picks up the words with a sneer: "This *lady*!" But Twemlow rebukes him angrily, "his wristbands bristling". It seems that Society is made to repent also.

Whether *The Mystery of Edwin Drood* would have turned out to be a novel of repentance also, we cannot know. But there is a hint given at the end of the opening chapter when John Jasper returns to the cathedral having spent the night at the Limehouse opium den. "The Sacristan locks the iron-barred gates . . . and all of the procession having scuttled into their places, hide their faces; and then the intoned words, 'WHEN THE WICKED MAN –' rise among groins of arches and beams of roof, awakening muttered thunder." The continuation of those intoned words is surely significant: "When the wicked man turneth away from his wickedness that he hath committed, and doeth that which is lawful and right, he shall save his soul alive." The quotation would have been very apt as a motto for *A Tale of Two Cities* or *Great Expectations*, but it raises problems when applied to *Edwin Drood*. Who was the wicked man? Was it necessarily John Jasper? And how was he to have saved his soul alive? Could it possibly be that someone else – Edwin Drood, perhaps – was the wicked man?

For several years Dickens published a special Christmas number of *All the Year Round*. Each number usually consisted of several independent chapters written around a unifying theme. Dickens would write one or two of these chapters, and the others would be contributed by fellow writers. In 1857, the Christmas number was *The Perils of Certain English Prisoners*, set in Central America but based loosely on events during the recent Indian Mutiny. Dickens wrote two of the three chapters and Wilkie Collins the other. The following year he contributed *Going into Society* which furnished him later with a popular reading, *Mr. Chops the Dwarf*. The Christmas numbers continued until 1867 and included the amusing *Mrs. Lirriper's Lodgings* in 1863, and *Mrs. Lirriper's Legacy* in 1864. The 1865 Christmas number, *Doctor Marigold's Prescriptions*, provided another popular reading, and *Mugby Junction* in 1866 contained Dickens' best ghost-story – *The Signalman*. His last

Christmas number was again written solely in conjunction with Wilkie
Collins. This was *No Thoroughfare*, which was dramatised by Collins
and staged with great success, both in England and France (where it
appeared under the title *L'Abîme*). Later it was equally successful in
America.

In addition to his Christmas Stories, Dickens collaborated with
Wilkie Collins in *The Lazy Tour of Two Idle Apprentices*, being an account
of their tour through Cumbria and North Yorkshire in the autumn of
1857. He also wrote three short works for American publishers. The
first, *Hunted Down*, appeared in the *New York Ledger* in 1859. This was
based on the life of Thomas Griffiths Wainwright, the notorious
poisoner. The second, *George Silverman's Explanation*, was published by
the *Atlantic Monthly* between January and March 1867. This slight piece
has recently aroused a great deal of interest because of its apparent
relevance to Dickens's inner "secret" life. "Upon myself, it has made the
strangest impression of reality and originality!!", Dickens confided to
Wills. "And I feel as if I had read something (by somebody else) which I
should never get out of my head!!" The third piece, *A Holiday Romance*,
containing stories for children, among them the popular *Magic Fishbone*,
appeared in *Our Young Folks*, a periodical published by Ticknor and
Fields. For each of these contributions to American markets, Dickens
was paid the incredible sum (for those days) of £1,000.

In our attempts to visualise Dickens at Gad's Hill, there is no doubt
that the most helpful of his writings are those essays in *The Uncommercial
Traveller* which deal with the Medway area. We learn a lot about
Dickens, his life at Gad's Hill, and his childhood recollections from
'Travelling Abroad', 'Tramps', 'Dullborough Town', 'Chatham Dock-
yard' and to a lesser extent from 'Birthday Celebrations'. It was in the
essay 'Travelling Abroad' that Dickens revealed his childhood admiration for Gad's Hill Place. In 'Dullborough Town' he described how
Rochester had appeared to him as a boy, and how it had since 'shrunk
fearfully'. But it is the essay on 'Tramps' which catches the feel of Gad's
Hill and its vicinity more intensely than any others. The reader is, so it
seems, invited to sit with Dickens at his desk in the library and look out
with him across the lawn.

"Yonder, by the high road, glaring white in the bright sunshine, lies,
on the dusty bit of turf under the bramble-bush that fences the coppice
from the highway, the tramp of the order savage, fast asleep," and "I
have my eye on a piece of Kentish wood, bordered on either side by a
wood."

Then Dickens invites his reader to accompany him outside – "say, on a road with a sea-breeze making its dust lively, and sails of ships in the blue distance beyond the slope of Dover." As he describes the various types of tramp one may encounter, he allows us to enter with him into the lives of some of them. "Among all the innumerable occupations that cannot possibly be transacted without the assistance of lookers on, chair-mending may take a station in the first rank. When we sat down with our backs against the barn or the public-house, and began to mend, what a sense of popularity would grow upon us!" And later, as he enters sympathetically into the life of the clockmender, he gives us a memorable picture of nearby Cobham Park and Hall. "Likewise we foresee great interest in going round by the park plantations, under the overhanging boughs (hares, rabbits, partridges, and pheasants scudding like mad across and across the chequered ground before us), and so over the park ladders." This introduces the reader to "the old Hall, solemn and grand" and the clockmender "insinuated with a candle into the stable-turret" where he would "work and work, until the day gradually turned to dusk, and even until the dusk gradually turned to dark. Our task at length accomplished, we should be taken into an enormous servants' hall, and there regaled with beef and bread, and powerful ale. Then, paid freely, we should be at liberty to go. . . . So should we lie that night at the ancient sign of the Crispin and Crispianus, and rise early next morning to be betimes on tramp again."

CHAPTER 8

Final Years

Despite his amazing displays of energy, his desire to be known as a fit man, capable of 20 mile walks and night-climbs up Carrick Fell when he could out-distance his companions, Dickens was in reality not particularly strong. He had been a sickly child and his boyhood experiences in the blacking warehouse had not helped him. There had been a memorable occasion when he had a bad "attack of spasm" in the warehouse. "I suffered such excruciating pain that time," he told Foster, "that they made a temporary bed of straw in my old recess in the counting-house, and I rolled about on the floor." One evening during this time he had an attack in his lodgings in Lant Street, where the compassionate landlord and his wife, with their son, stood anxiously about his bed until morning. In 1845, while in Italy, he had a nasty mishap one night when running to get back into Genoa before the town gates were closed. It being so dark, he failed to see a pole across the road, and fell over it, injuring himself, and probably (as some authorities have conjectured) damaging his kidneys.

His letters are sprinkled with references to his heavy colds, sore throats, swollen faces, rheumatism and to feeling "so very unwell this morning, with giddiness, and headache and botheration of one sort or other" (1 Nov 1845). Clearly, he had not enjoyed the best of health for a long time before ever coming to Gad's Hill Place, and in the last decade of his life his health was to deteriorate sharply.

Towards the end of February 1865, Dickens began to complain of a frost-bitten foot. He wrote to Forster:

"I got frost-bitten by walking continually in the snow, and getting wet in the feet daily. My boots hardened and softened, hardened and softened, my left foot swelled, and I still forced the boot on; sat in it to write, half the day; walked in it through the snow, the other half; forced the boot on again next morning; sat and walked again; and being accustomed to all sorts of changes in my feet, took no heed. At length, going out as usual, I fell lame on the walk, and had to limp home dead lame, through the snow, for the last three miles – to the remarkable terror, by-the-bye, of the two big dogs."

This letter reveals the sort of bravado which Dickens indulged in. This boasting of how he forced his boot on, and took no heed of the swelling, but continued to write half the day and walk in the snow the other half, is a sorry example of a great man's stupidity. He had a duty to take better care of himself. Instead, he bragged of what poor care he had taken.

The foot was not easily cured. In March, Dickens moved to 16 Somers Place, Hyde Park, which he had rented for the spring. He wrote to Layard on 16th March to report that he had been laid up with the foot and "suffered tortures". On 25th March, he told his doctor "Here is this confounded foot as bad as ever again. I suffered tortures all last night, and never closed my eyes. We are now at work at the Poppy fomentation again." And to another correspondent, he wrote that same date: "I have been unwell for some days." Indeed, this first attack of trouble with his foot was not wholly over by the end of April. "My frost-bitten foot," he told Macready, on 22nd April, "after causing me great inconvenience and much pain, has begun to conduct itself amiably. I can now again walk my 10 miles in the morning without inconvenience, but am absurdly obliged to sit shoeless all the evening.– a very slight penalty as I detest going out to dinner. . . ." Five days later, he wrote to Fredrick Lehmann: "Today I am going out to dinner for the first time. But whether I can keep a boot on, and get it on again for the Academy Dinner on Saturday, remains to be seen." His foot, unfortunately, was to trouble him more and more seriously for the remainder of his life.

But he was to suffer another extremely serious blow to his constitution on 9th June of that year. Owing to an incredible lack of communication between the railway operators and their repair gangs, the line was taken up at Staplehurst ahead of the train in which Dickens, Ellen Ternan and her mother were travelling from Dover to London. There was a dreadful disaster. Most of the train fell into the stream below, while Dickens' carriage hung over the ruined brickwork. Dickens was able to clamber out and attend to the injured amidst frightful scenes of death and destruction. Ten passengers were killed, and the shock Dickens sustained was not easily overcome. For some days his shaky hand could hardly hold a pen. And ever after, whenever he was travelling by train, he had a dread of a similar accident happening. Forster culled successive bulletins from his letters at this time:

"I am curiously weak – weak as if I were recovering from a long illness" . . . "I begin to feel it more in my head. I sleep well and eat well: but I write half a dozen notes, and turn faint and sick" . . . "I am getting right, though still low in pulse and very nervous. Driving into Rochester yesterday I felt more shaken than I have since the accident" . . . "I cannot bear railway travelling yet. A perfect conviction, against the senses, that the carriage is down on one side (and generally that is the left, and *not* the side on which the carriage in the accident really went over), comes upon me with anything like speed, and is inexpressibly distressing."

As the 1860's progressed, however, Dickens chose to make more and more railway journeys, even though, as he said on arriving in Edinburgh from London in December 1868, he calculated that a journey over such a distance involved something more than 30,000 shocks to the nerves! He complained of his watch ceasing to keep accurate time following the accident. But it was not only his watch that had been affected.

On 8th February 1866, his doctor, Frank Beard, gave him a thorough medical examination. Dickens had written to tell him that he feared his pulse was behaving erratically, so Beard insisted that an examination of the heart was absolutely necessary. Dickens had already suspected some heart trouble and was not surprised to learn that there seemed to be degeneration of some of its functions. He told his sister-in-law: "It does not contract as it should. So I have got a prescription of iron, quinine, and digitalis, to set it a-going, and send the blood more quickly through the system. If it should not seem to succeed on a reasonable trial, I will then propose a consultation with someone else. Of course, I am not so foolish to suppose that all my work can have been achieved without *some* penalty, and I have noticed for some time a decided change in my buoyancy and hopefulness – in other words, in my usual 'tone'." A second opinion by Dr. William Brinton of Bush Street, was that his trouble was "only remarkable irritability of the heart". Perhaps this assurance and the belief that tonics had already "brought him round", allowed Dickens to go ahead that same month and accept "an offer from Chappells of Bond Street, of £50 a night for 30 nights to read 'in England, Ireland, Scotland, or Paris.'" There was to be no restraining the man!

The readings took place as arranged from April to July. Dickens suffered from a cold for much of that time. In Clifton he was "not at all well" as he informed his sister-in-law. In Perth, he reported that he was "in a condition the reverse of flourishing: half strangled with my cold, and dyspeptically gloomy and dull." After the readings were over, however, he confessed to Frank Beard: "I have been bothered for weeks, months, at intervals, with distension and flatulency, and disagreeable pains in the pit of the stomach and chest, without any disarrangement of the bowels, worth speaking of. Sometimes I have it all day, sometimes at capricious intervals, sometimes all night after 2 or so." Later that month (September 1866) he told Foster: "Twice last week I was seized in a most distressing manner – apparently in the heart; but I am persuaded, only in the nervous system." Other troubles were also besetting him – haemorrhoids which were to become increasingly troublesome and lead to embarrassing haemorrhages on more than one occasion – and varicose veins for which he obtained surgical stockings.

Yet despite these accumulating physical problems, in the midst of discomfort and sleeplessness, Dickens was nursing the idea of making a reading tour of the United States. The idea had been sown by his American friend, the publisher James T. Fields. Yet although Dickens replied on 2nd May 1866 that he did not know "that any sum of money . . . would induce me to cross the Atlantic . . .", he was to be tempted by a large offer made in July, and a year later was making detailed plans for the tour. On 9th November 1867, he set sail from Liverpool for Boston.

The American tour netted Dickens a large sum of money (over £19,000) but the penalty was excessive. He did not return home until 2nd May, 1868, having given 75 readings and travelled hundreds of miles up and down the railway lines between Boston, New York, Philadelphia, Washington and Baltimore. In December he began to suffer from a heavy cold which remained with him, and although he joked about "the true American catarrh", and swallowed the "Rocky Mountain Sneezer" (made of rum, brandy and snow) which was "guaranteed" to cure it, the cold and cough could not be moved. It was terrible weather. Coming to New York in December, Dickens found the temperature several degrees below zero, and snow was some eight inches deep, making transport difficult. The weather remained bad throughout his visit, and he was forced to stay in his hotel rooms for much of the time. On the frequent rail journeys, however, he suffered not only from the fear of another Staplehurst, but from the stuffy carriages and the wild weather outside. "You are one of, say, a hundred people in a heated car with a great stove in it, all the little windows being closed, and the bumping and banging about are indescribable, the atmosphere detestable, and ordinary motion all but intolerable," he told his eldest daughter, while to his eldest son he wrote: "The railway journeys distress me greatly. I get out into the open air (upon the break), and it snows and blows, and the train bumps, and the steam flies at me until I am driven in again." Then, to add to his troubles, his foot began to pain him again. Dolby, his manager, wrote later:

"This he ascribed to walking about at Niagara in the snow. Up to this time the illness was confined to the left foot, but symptoms now presented themselves of an attack in the right foot also, and caused him to be lame for the remainder of the time he was in America. Still," continued Dolby, "he persevered with the task he had before him, and performed it without one word of complaint, all the time; seldom eating and drinking, and scarcely ever sleeping."

Dickens arrived back at Gad's Hill on 2nd May 1868, and was given the enthusiastic welcome described in an earlier chapter. The sea voyage, though rough, had apparently done wonders for his health. He told Macready that "Katie, Mary and Georgina expected a wreck, and were, at first, much mortified", and he wrote to an American friend "I sank my American catarrh in the Atlantic on the fourth day out, and disappointed all my friends by landing in the brownest and most radiant health." This was hardly the entire truth, and he had to confess to his old friend in Switzerland, Monsieur De Cerjat, to being a little fatigued since his return. Nevertheless, he was planning another series of readings in the United Kingdom. His letter went on to say:

"My escape in the Staplehurst accident of three years ago is not to be obliterated from my nervous system. To this hour I have sudden vague rushes of terror, even when riding in a hansom cab, which are perfectly unreasonable but quite insurmountable. I used to make nothing of driving a pair of horses habitually through the most crowded parts of London, I cannot now drive, with comfort to myself, on the country roads here; and I doubt if I could ride at all in the saddle. My reading secretary and companion knows so well when one of these odd momentary seizures comes upon me in a railway carriage, that he instantly produces a dram of brandy, which rallies the blood to the heart and generally prevails."

While he had been in America, he had been distressed to learn of the death of an old friend, the Rev. Chauncey Hare Townshend, who had once addressed a sonnet to Dickens, calling him "Man of the genial mind" whose "vigorous hand ... turns with master-care the mighty engine of the popular mind to indignation." Dickens had a great fondness for Townshend, although he had none for Townshend's dog, Bully. In 1859, Dickens had not looked forward with any pleasure to Townshend's coming to stay at Gad's Hill if he were bringing Bully with him. He told Cerjat: "Townshend is severely treated by Bully who rules him with a paw of iron." But on receiving news of Townshend's death, Dickens was greatly upset. "I never, never, never was better loved by a man than I was by him, I am sure. Poor dear fellow, good affectionate gentle creature."

Townshend left Dickens £1,000 and appointed him "his literary executor" to publish his "religious opinions". When Dickens returned from America he found the mass of Townshend's papers delivered to him. His heart sank as he saw what 'an extraordinarily difficult task' lay ahead for him. He wrote to the solicitor: "I presume that the cost of its printing and publication will be paid by the estate. No bookseller would entertain the notion of buying it, or taking the risk of it, I am certain. And I doubt whether a score of copies will ever get into public circulation." However, Dickens had promised to do what he could. So, in the midst of his work as editor and public reader, he set about sorting the "dispersed fragments, originally written in pencil, afterward inked over" ... and the "journals of travel, fragments of poems, critical essays, voluminous correspondence, and old school-exercises and college themes, having no kind of connection with them." Finally, in 1869 "The Religious Opinions of the late Rev. Chauncey Hare Townshend, ed. C.D." appeared in print. Today, copies of it are as rare as they are uninteresting.

During these later years it is clear that Dickens was not at Gad's Hill as often as is generally believed and that Georgina and Mamie must have spent many days there without him. His reading engagements took him all over the country and three times to Ireland. There were intervals between these tours, of course, and even during the tours he usually managed to return home for odd days and weekends. His most prolonged absence was his American tour which lasted for six months from November 1867 to the beginning of May 1868. From its founding in 1859 he was "conducting" his journal *All the Year Round*, and this necessitated attendance at the office as frequently as possible. He therefore had to be in London a great deal, and while in town he had theatres, dinners, and other social events to attend. Very often he found these engagements ended too late to permit him to travel back to Higham. So he would stay the night in the flat above the journal's office in Wellington Street.

During the 1860's it became his practice to take a house for the London season, ostensibly to permit his daughter, Mamie, to enjoy the social round (and possibly find herself a husband). In 1861 he took a house in Hanover Terrace, Regent's Park. In 1862 he exchanged houses for three months with a friend, and moved into 16 Hyde Park Gate. For three successive years – 1864, 1865 and 1866–he took other houses in the Hyde Park neighbourhood for similar periods, but did not do so again until 1870 when he rented 5 Hyde Park Place.

In his final decade he had several short holidays. He made a tour of Cornwall in November 1860. He stayed at the Royal Warden Hotel in Dover once or twice, and went to see friends occasionally, such as Bulwer Lytton at Knebworth where he stayed in June 1861. There were visits abroad. He went to France in June 1862, and from October to just before Christmas that year went backwards and forwards across the Channel. He was back in Paris on 15th January 1863 and read at the British Embassy before setting out on a tour of Northern France lasting until late February. In June 1864 he took another holiday abroad, and from his mention of a 'Mysterious Disappearance', it might be inferred that he went with Ellen Ternan to Condette. He was again in France during May 1865, and it was while he was travelling back to London with Ellen and her mother that he was involved in the accident at Staplehurst on 9th June.

Finally there were various occasions when it seems he was visiting Ellen Ternan at her home in Slough. After May 1867, Ellen apparently moved to Windsor Lodge, Peckham, and Dickens visited her there. But his visits are not documented, and one can only conjecture when and how frequently they took place. It would seem, however, that like his visits to Gad's Hill, his visits to Ellen were rather fewer than people imagine.

In the last ten years, Dickens completed only two novels and wrote half of another. As was shown in the last chapter, his literary output was in no way comparable to that between 1836 and 1841, but it was not insignificant, and his total work-load was crippling, especially from 1868 onwards. While Dickens was in America his assistant editor, W.H.

Wills, had met with a serious accident in the hunting field. This meant that on his return home, Dickens had to take an even greater share in the conduct of *All The Year Round*. At the same time, he was met with a mountain of correspondence plus the miscellaneous collection of Townshend's Opinions. It was not surprising that he should be "overwhelmed with business" nor, despite his breezy remarks about his health and his doctor's exclamation that he looked some seven years younger, that the toll on his strength, exacted by the American trip, should soon be manifest. But he would not abandon his plans for another series of 72 readings for £80 a performance. Hardly had he begun them, however, than there were signs once more of trouble with his feet. Now the right foot also was being affected. During the first month of reading, he had to confess to Foster that he had not been well.

Characteristically, Dickens had taken little rest between his return home and the opening reading in London on 5th October 1868. He had been across to Paris almost immediately after his return in order to supervise the staging of the French version of *No Thoroughfare*, entitled *L'Âbime*. A cartoon published at this time showed Dickens stepping heedlessly through an open trap-door on the stage, surely prophetic of the abyss into which his eagerness both to make money and to win applause was leading him. During that summer he gave a series of parties, and Dolby recorded:

"there was not a week when he did not entertain those friends whose society afforded him so much pleasure. The early days of the week were devoted to business purposes; Mr. Dickens, on these days, taking up his residence at the office in London, returning to Gad's with his guests, as a rule, on Friday, and remaining there until the following Monday, when all returned to London together in a saloon carriage."

Dickens now conceived the idea of devising a new reading – the "Murder of Nancy" from *Oliver Twist*. He read it over to Dolby and gave an outline to Forster. Both of them advised against his proceeding with it, but for opposite reasons. Dolby who had no objection to its content, felt it would be too great a strain on Dickens' health, while Forster, giving too little weight to the health hazard, considered "such a subject ... to be altogether out of the province of reading." Yet Forster subsequently recorded: "In the intervals of my official work I saw him frequently that summer, and never without the impression that America had told heavily upon him. There was manifest abatement of his natural force, the elasticity of bearing was impaired, and the wonderful brightness of eye was dimmed at times. One day, too, as he walked from his office with Miss Hogarth to dine at our house, he could read only the halves of the letters over the shop doors that were on his right as he looked." But these symptoms, like the catarrh which had been such a trial in America, vanished when he was called upon to make a special exertion. Few people realised what danger he was in.

Performance of the "Murder of Nancy" reading was to prove a tremendous strain. He gave a trial performance on 14th November to an invited audience of about 100, and then on 5th January 1869 it was given the first of its 28 public performances. Its effect upon audiences was astounding. At Clifton "from a dozen to twenty ladies were taken out stiff and rigid, at various times". The effect upon Dickens was disastrous. His pulse rate soared and he was left prostrated and exhausted when he came off the stage.

The series of readings, especially the "Murder", and continual travel rapidly undermined Dickens' health. On 16th February 1869 his medical advisors (who now included Sir Henry Thompson) insisted that the London reading planned for that evening should be cancelled and that he should not travel to Edinburgh on the following day. He managed to continue, however, after a brief rest, but was on the platform again on 20th February. So the whirligig when on – Wolverhampton, Manchester, York, Ipswich, Cambridge – until eventually on 19th April he found himself in Blackburn feeling so ill that he was compelled to complain to Dr. Beard of being "extremely giddy, extremely uncertain of my footing (especially of the left side) and extremely indisposed to raise my hands to my head.". Beard realised how serious this was and on 22nd April he came up to Preston. Dickens was all set to go and read that evening but Beard, after giving him a thorough examination in the hotel, told Dolby: "If you insist on Dickens taking the platform tonight, I will not guarantee but that he goes through life dragging a foot after him." This series, therefore, ended abruptly and Dickens returned to London and eventually to Gad's Hill.

Throughout this worrying time, especially after the weekend he had spent in Chester prior to going to Blackburn when it is possible that during the night he suffered a slight stroke, he had prevented any real information about his condition reaching Georgina and Mamie. He pleaded to Forster: "Don't say anything in the Gad's direction about my being a little out of sorts. I have broached the matter, of course; but very lightly."

So, for a while, Dickens resumed his life of shuttling between Gad's Hill and the office of *All The Year Round*. His American friends, James T. Fields and Annie, came to London and Mamie and Georgina stayed with Dickens at the St. James' Hotel in Piccadilly in order to escort the visitors around London, take them to Windsor, and dine with them at the Star and Garter, Richmond. Then, on 2nd June, the Fields came to Gad's Hill and Dickens organised the delightful excursions about the Kent countryside which have been described in Chapter 5.

The desire to resume his career as a reader could not be overcome. Sir Henry Thompson some five or six weeks after the Preston cancellation had given his consent for a final series of readings, provided they involved no travelling. So on 11th January 1870 Dickens was again on the platform, and gave twelve readings at St. James' Hall, London. (The Meridien Hotel now stands on the site.) The readings were enthusiastically supported, and large crowds had to be turned away. Once again, Dickens was placed under a tremendous strain. At times he showed symptoms of not being fully in command of his words. His son noticed an inability occasionally to pronounce Mr. Pickwick's name correctly. Nor was he able to relax properly on his days off. On 9th March he was received in audience by Queen Victoria. The Clerk of the Privy Council, Mr (later Sir) Arthur Helps, had arranged the interview, prior to which he evidently conveyed to Dickens confidential information about a proposition for a further indication of royal approval. In a letter dated 3rd March 1870, Dickens replied: "My Dear Helps, We will have 'Of Gad's Hill Place' attached to the title of the Baronetcy, please – on account of the divine William and Falstaff. . . ."

But this excitement was nothing compared with that of the Farewell Reading on 15th March. He read two of his favourite pieces that evening – *A Christmas Carol* and "The Trial" from *Pickwick*. St. James' Hall was packed to capacity with 2,000 people, and the applause when the reading was over was tumultuous and prolonged. Dickens came back onto the platform to acknowledge the genuine display of love which his public bore him, and to make a brief, but undoubtedly his most memorable speech, concluding: "From these garish lights I vanish now for ever more, with a heart-felt, grateful, respectful, affectionate farewell."

Dickens should then have been able to get down to Gad's Hill and really unwind. This was the opportunity to walk out with his dogs, or sit in his easy chair and perhaps read Carlyle's *French Revolution* for the

501st time. At least he might have finished at leisure Arthur Helps' *Life of Columbus* which had just been published, and was perhaps the book he had told its author he was currently reading 'with great pleasure'. But there was too much to do. He had to attend a royal levée wearing the blue suit ornamented with gold braid which may still be seen at No. 48 Doughty Street, London. He had to preside at the dinner of the Newsvendors' Benevolent Institution, speak at the Royal Academy banquet, and attend dinners at Lord Stanhope's and Dean Stanley's. There were other social events – breakfast at the Prime Minister's (Mr. Gladstone's), theatre with Lady Molesworth, and a reception and supper at his own apartments in Hyde Park Place at which there was a brilliant gathering of celebrities. He also lavished all his care for detail, all his knowledge of the theatre, on the private theatricals being arranged by his London neighbours. Dickens took charge of all rehearsals, and demonstrated in a "master class" how the actors and actresses should move and speak and conduct themselves. Unfortunately, his foot was still giving exquisite pain, or he would have acted one of the parts himself. As it was, his two daughters were in the production, for which Millais had painted the scenery. On 2nd June, the play was presented with Dickens as stage manager and prompter. It was a fitting last night in London.

So at last Dickens arrived at Gad's Hill, keen to get down to work on the next instalment of *Edwin Drood*, the first part of which had been published on 1st April. He was now able to enjoy the new conservatory, although he was apprehensive that it might have been extravagantly expensive. Georgina had supervised the purchase and planting out of new beds of geraniums being careful (on her brother-in-law's instructions) not to spend too much on them. So everything was bright and fresh. The weather was warm. *Drood* was selling splendidly. But Dickens was no longer his old self.

Katey came down to Gad's Hill on Sunday, 5th June, and she at once noticed a "greyness" about her father's face which rather alarmed her. She had come to seek his advice about an offer she had received to make the stage her career. However her father would not discuss it until the other members of the family had gone to bed and Katey and he could talk together alone. Dickens seemed better at dinner, and the conversation was lively and entertaining. Afterwards, he smoked a cigar as usual, and when Georgina and Mamie had retired, father and daughter settled down comfortably to discuss the topic on which she was so keen to learn his opinion. She was no doubt disappointed at the earnestness with which he opposed her proposition. "You are too sensitive," he told her. "Although there are nice people on the stage, there are some who would make your hair stand on end." They went on to discuss all sorts of other things. Dickens said he wished he had been "a better father – a better man". And so they talked on and on, and when they finally made their way upstairs it was 3 o'clock in the morning.

The following day, Mamie was to accompany Katey back to London for a few days. Before they left, Katey went to the chalet to say good-bye to her father who was then busily writing *Edwin Drood*. She remembered later that contrary to his usual habit of offering her his cheek to be kissed, he kissed her very affectionately. She bade him good-bye and was on her way down the tunnel steps, when suddenly she felt the urge to go back again. She did so, climbed up the stairs of the chalet, and knocked on his door. When he called to her to enter, she ran in. He turned to face her and opened his arms to embrace her once more. They said nothing, but kissed one another emotionally before she tore herself away for the last time.

On the 6th and 7th June, Dickens continued to work on the next part of *Edwin Drood*, and on the latter day took a drive into Cobham Park. On 8th June he was so anxious to complete the instalment that he decided to carry on working after lunch, which was not his usual habit. At about 1 o'clock therefore he returned to the house for a short break, and smoked a cigar in the conservatory before resuming his labours in the chalet. That afternoon he must have written the memorable paragraph:

> "A brilliant morning shines on the old city. Its antiquities and ruins are surpassingly beautiful, with the lusty ivy gleaming in the sun, and the rich trees waving in the balmy air. Changes of glorious light from moving boughs, songs of birds, scents from gardens, woods, and fields – or, rather, from the one great garden of the whole cultivated island in its yielding time – penetrate into the Cathedral, subdue its earthy odour, and preach the Resurrection and the Life. The cold stone tombs of centuries ago grow warm; and flecks of brightness dart into the sternest marble corners of the building, fluttering there like wings."

And having described Datchery sitting down to "a very neat clean breakfast" and falling to "with an appetite", Dickens laid down his pen and left the chalet for ever.

Back in the house he wrote several letters before dinner was served. It was then that Georgina noticed a marked change in him. She asked if he were ill, and he replied that he was – and had been for the last hour. Georgina wanted to send for a doctor, but Dickens refused to allow her. His remarks then became rambling and incoherent – about the sale of a neighbour's property, and the whereabout of Macready's son – until he declared he must set out for London immediately and staggered to his feet. He could hardly stand, and Georgina quickly came to his side and upheld him, trying to get him to the sofa. "On the ground," muttered Dickens, and those were his last words.

Though the local doctor and the medical specialists from London came to attend him, Dickens lay unconscious all that night, and most of the following day. At 6.10 pm on the evening of 9th June, he breathed his last.

Postscript

The Dean and Chapter of Rochester Cathedral had plans to bury him in their Cathedral, but deferred to Westminster's wish to lay him to rest in a place so rich in the heritage of our history.

But I believe – I am sure – he would have preferred to lie in a little peaceful and secluded Kentish garden where the wild flowers mingle with the grass and a light wind strews it with beautiful shadows of clouds and moves the blossom in the trees whilst the larks sing high above.

Yet he would be content and must have been thrilled to know that so many of his friends, the people, had come with their flowers to say goodbye in Westminster Abbey.

His wishes had been carried out with great care. At six o'clock on the morning of 14th June a plain coffin left Gad's Hill and was brought in a special train to Charing Cross. There it was removed to a hearse without feathers or any funeral trappings. Three coaches only followed it to the Abbey. All was still as the little cortege swept round the Broad Sanctuary and drove under the archway. Then, a moment later, the great bell began tolling. Through the western cloister door the body was conveyed along the nave into the South Transept, the Poets' Corner. Here, the night before, a grave had been dug. In the peacefulness and silence of the shadowy arches the brief words of the burial service were said. There were no choristers, but at the end the organ played a Dead March. Last to turn away, when all was over, was a burly man tightly buttoned up in a black frock coat, who could not trust himself to speak. But John Forster, even in his grief, noted with pride that the monuments of Chaucer, Shakespeare, Dryden, and David Garrick surrounded the grave of his friend.

On the following Sunday, Dean Stanley said:

"If any of you have learnt from his works the eternal value of generosity, purity, kindness, unselfishness, and have learnt to show these in your own hearts and lives, these are the best monuments, memorials and testimonials of one who loved with a rare and touching love, his friends, his country, and his fellow men."

Those three words – "monuments, memorials, and testimonials" – also appeared in Dickens' will:

"I emphatically direct that I be buried in an inexpensive, unostentatious and strictly private manner; and that no public announcement be made of the time or place of my burial and at the utmost not more than three plain mourning coaches be employed, and those who attend my funeral wear no scarf, black bow, long hat band or other such revolting absurdity. I direct that my name be inscribed in plain English letters on my tomb without the addition of Mr or Esq. I conjure my friends on no account to make me the subject of any monument, memorial or testimonial whatever. I rest my claims to the remembrance of my country upon my published works."

Cedric Charles Dickens

GUINNESS WAS GOOD
FOR THEM

THAT " PHIZ " should have drawn Sam Weller writing his Valentine in front of a Guinness placard shows how much a part of the background of life Guinness had become by 1837.

Guinness had probably reached England towards the end of the 18th century, when it had already been brewed in Dublin for nearly forty years. It had quickly become at home in every level of society, and as much a part of everyday life then as it is for us.

GUINNESS IS GOOD FOR YOU

This advertisement appeared in the Spring 1955 Dickensian